BODY

BUSINESS 2.0

USING
Nonverbal Communication
FOR BUSINESS SUCCESS

Other books by Ken Cooper:

- *Taming the Terrible Too's of Training* (with Dan Cooper)
- *Stop It Now: How targets and managers can end sexual harassment*
- *The Relational Enterprise*
- *Effective Competency Modeling and Reporting*
- *Always Bear Left ... and other ways to get things done faster and easier*
- *The World's Greatest Blackjack Book* (with Lance Humble)
- *Body Business: Using Nonverbal Communication for Business Success*

Updated edition, originally published as:
- *Nonverbal Communication for Business Success*
- *Body Business: The sender's and receiver's guide to nonverbal communication*
- *Kroppspråket–Din Genväg Till Framgång* (Liber)
- *Communicacion No Verbal Para Ejecutivos* (Interamericana)

BODY

BUSINESS 2.0

USING
Nonverbal Communication
FOR BUSINESS SUCCESS

Ken Cooper

TotalComm Press

St. Louis

This publication is designed to provide accurate and authoritative information in regard to the subject matter covered. It is sold with the understanding that the publisher is not engaged in rendering legal, accounting, or other professional service. If legal advice or other expert assistance is required, the services of a competent professional person should be sought.

ISBN: 978-0-9850949-6-6

All names, companies, brands, products, and services mentioned in this book are the trade names or registered trademarks of their respective owners.

Book design: Peggy Nehmen. This book is set in Latino URW and Gotham.

First AMACOM hardback edition 1979.
First AMACOM trade paperback edition 1981.
Printed in the United States of America.

KenCooper.com

To Sue, Jeff, Dan and Mara

Contents

Notes on the 2.0 Edition

THIS IS THE FIRST BOOK to ever take the social "hot topic" concept of body language and scientifically apply it to the workplace. Writing it was a labor of love that ended up paying off for decades. Now, with the new online publishing and print-on-demand options available, it's time to make *Body Business* available again.

To begin, a little background...

My wife and I married after my junior year at the University of Missouri. She helped put me through my senior and graduate years in Industrial Engineering at the University of Missouri. After I graduated, I got a job at IBM selling mainframe computer systems to regulated utilities.

My training at IBM was quite extensive, but it focused primarily on technology and sales call skills. If I was going to be successful and differentiate myself from other sales reps, I had to learn more about being a successful communicator.

Now that I had a job, my wife could go back to school and complete her degree program. Without anything like the internet in those days, that meant spending long hours at various libraries in town. So that we could be together, I'd go with her and research topics that went beyond my IBM training—subjects such as presentation skills, memory improvement, creativity, conflict management, and yes, nonverbal communication (NVC) or "body language" as it was known then.

I became particularly interested in the potential of this body language topic. It felt like an extension of the study of human movements from my Industrial Engineering training. And the scientific approach to understanding the various nonverbal rules appealed to me. So I began to read everything I could find on anything related to nonverbal communication. In fact, I did more research on this subject than I did for my Master's degree. In the end, I had this massive amount of raw data about NVC signals and relationships.

The problem was, at the time, there was only one approach to NVC. This was promoted by Julius Fast in his best-selling book, *Body Language.* The cover showed an attractive woman sitting with her legs crossed, with captions such as, "Does her body say she's a loose woman?" and "Does her body say that she's a manipulator?" It was all social pseudo-science. And it promoted a "this means that" philosophy, i.e., one signal directly means one trait.

It was clear from my research, and from my work and life experience, that this was absolutely wrong. One signal, taken out of context, without any sort of other supporting signs, means nothing.

Take the arms-crossed pose. It's supposed to be a negative sign, a form of covering up. Yet it's a habitual gesture for many people. Maybe they're cold. Maybe their underarms itch. Who knows? But the point is, unless there are other nonverbals indicating a similar trait, then you have nothing reliable to work with.

So I began to develop a "correlated read" approach where you scan a number of related factors, and draw a conclusion when you have multiple indicators in agreement. This way you generate a *reliable* read that you can interpret and act on for your benefit. This resulted in the three scans highlighted in this book—**the body position scan, (proxemics), the indicators scan (artifacts), and the body movement scan (kinesics).**

I found that using these scans opened up a whole new world of communication. I was finally "listening with my eyes open." There was a lot of information that I might have been subliminally reacting to. But now I was consciously looking for and interpreting all this NVC that had always been available, but that I hadn't been using.

As a result, *Body Business* has changed my life, and has hopefully helped others become more effective in theirs. It made me a better salesman. It made me a better speaker, trainer, educator, and consultant. It made me a better husband and father. And it has made interacting with others in life much more interesting.

I explain to people that it's like going from watching black-and-white video to viewing in color. The same information is there if you look hard enough for it. There's just so much more depth and insight when you consciously add NVC to the mix.

Body Business also changed my life professionally. In the intervening years since this book was first published, I've continued to tap into the growing research on NVC. I've spoken to over 1,000 audiences on NVC as applied to leadership, sales, service, and communication. I've coached individuals and teams. My NVC speech has been captured on video and audio by The International Program Source and by McGraw-Hill respectively. I've appeared in online video training programs for ej4.com, and have written a video-based NVC series for BizLibrary. I've tutored political candidates for the U.S. Senate and House on presentation skills. I've provided on-air presidential debate analysis for a TV network affiliate. I've appeared on national radio and TV talk show programs. I've used NVC concepts to provide additional insights into the prevention of sexual harassment. It's been quite a ride.

At this point, here are two questions you probably have about this book:

"It's 40 years old. The world has changed quite a bit. Is this still valid?"

That's a fair question. The answer is a strong "Yes!"

The world has definitely changed over the decades. Technology, styles, design, personal preferences, and so on, are certainly different. But interestingly, what hasn't changed is how people communicate. The research behind the NVC scans is as applicable as the day it was done. I'm still using these exact scans every day.

Your second question may be, "So what have you done with this new edition?"

This is not a re-write of *Body Business*, for the reason just given. It didn't need to be rewritten for today's workplace. This is an update.

Social sensibilities have changed. Technology has progressed. Some stories were no longer applicable or germane. Some references were too dated. So only minor changes were made, as needed. Otherwise, the content remains the same, and the editing remains consistent with the original AMACOM business writing style.

So here, once again in print, direct from the author, is the book that was the first to take the social topic of "body language" and convert it into a reliable technique that could be used to improve your business communication and performance—Body Business.

Ken Cooper
2020

Preface

I ALWAYS SAVE WRITING the Preface to a book for last. As I sit here and glance over the completed manuscript, freshly stacked in its box, I feel a strange sense of loss. *Nonverbal Communication for Business Success* contains some of my best material, up to now shared only for my speaking and training audiences. But I know it represents a milestone in the application of nonverbal communication to business.

Nonverbal communication involves the study of all parts of the communications process except words—body appearance and position, body movements, possessions, surroundings, and voice characteristics. I have used nonverbal communication to advantage both in my career as a computer salesman and now as a management consultant.

To date, there have been two main types of books about nonverbal communication: the technical research volume and the "secrets of body language" book.

The technical books are filled with fascinating studies identifying behavior and causes, but they are written for the academic community in language unintelligible to the average reader. The "secrets of body language" books have been immensely popular, but they make a fatal error in assigning specific meanings to individual body signals that are taken out of context. There are a few books that present the valuable research in a readable format. And up to now, no books have been designed primarily for use by the vast working public.

Nonverbal Communication for Business Success is that book. It introduces three visual "scans" that will help you systematically observe and analyze nonverbal information, and develop a reliable, correlated read. The scans will enable you to determine whether many different signs agree before you make a decision. You can find out how to choose a restaurant for a business lunch, learn why you should look away briefly when you meet someone, and see why wearing high heels ruins your walk.

The information presented in this book is the result of nearly ten years of research into the professional literature and an equal number of years of research and experience as a teacher and management consultant. It is not an abstract theory. However, no concept has been included unless it has been proven to me in personal practice, no matter what the research.

The book is not solely intended for those who work. It also contains chapters on effective voice traits and on developing a successful personal image. In the chapter on image, for example, you can see how important appearance was in the 1960 and 1976 presidential debates. I have even had students use the image-building process as parents and spouses.

Now is the time for you to find out what you have been missing. Now is the time for you to transact a little "body business."

Ken Cooper
1981

Acknowledgements

I WISH TO THANK:

Elmer Kowal for his photographic assistance.

Monsanto Company for the use of its facilities in the photograph sessions.

Shirley Dingler for obtaining permission for the sessions. Don Verbeck for making all session arrangements.

Jim Jones of IBM, and Juanita Carter, Kathy Lowes, Dr. John Mason, Frank Miller, George Panian, Bernie Phillips, Jim Spinks, Bob Stuckey, Don Verbeck, and Iniss Taylor—all of Monsanto Company—for posing for the illustrations.

Karen Gentles for manuscript preparation.

And all those friends and strangers who so graciously and patiently allowed me to try things out with them and observe them.

CHAPTER 1

Nonverbal Communication and Business

IT WOULD BE WONDERFUL if a secret Eastern society existed to teach us the mysteries of effective communication. We might click on a small coupon on our favorite website, spend "Only $2.99" of our PayPal credit, and wait expectantly for the Ancient Wisdom Parchment to arrive.

Knowing help was on the way, we could endure our communications failures. At last, the scroll would be sure to save us. Opening the plain–wrapped package with nervous anticipation, we would finally have the answers to the most perplexing problems in human relationships.

What would the message be?

Most likely, the parchment would not offer any deep secrets to successful communication—because there are none. Instead, it would probably contain certain communication techniques that all researchers in the field agree on.

This book provides such information for a special category of communication: *the nonverbals*. Much of what you read here may be intuitively obvious. But some information will be totally new. And some will seem to contradict what you always thought to be true.

For information you already know, you will learn more effective applications. For new information, you will find that you have been watching a digital color TV program in analog black and white. Where the forest is alive with sound, you have heard only the clump of your own footsteps. For contradictions, you will experience growth in your ability to communicate effectively.

In all three cases, you will learn the why of key nonverbal communication principles. You will become a conscious participant in a process that has been a subconscious part of your behavior every waking hour. That is, you will learn how to analyze the nonverbal signals being sent to you, and how to modify or control the nonverbal information you project.

Most people who have attained even moderate success in the business world have some ability to observe and evaluate nonverbals. For example, examine the three pictures in Figure 1–1. In each case, with whom is this salesman speaking?

A salesman at my first job invariably assumed these three postures when talking on the phone, never realizing that each one indicated clearly whether or not he was working. He adopted the first pose with a customer or another employee; the second, with a friend or casual business acquaintance, such as his broker. The third was usually reserved for one of his "close friends," since he was a bachelor. (If you said "business associate" for the first pose and "wife" for the second, I want to know who the third person is!)

As this phone example shows, we can make fairly accurate observations in a simple social situation. In more complex settings, however, we may become confused about nonverbal signals. As a first step in overcoming this difficulty, we should examine some of the communications basics that our brown wrapper book may have missed.

Communication Basics

To begin, there are four key concepts that can help us better understand any communications process. The first is that we communicate *with* someone, *not* to someone.

Communication is not necessarily taking place just because one person is talking to another. We frequently assume that it is, until we find that our listener is a million miles away. In an article in *Reader's Digest,* Carol Burnett tells a story about a conversation with her seven-year-old daughter after a spanking:

Figure 1–1. Phone conversation positions

"At bedtime, she was still sniffling," Carol recalled. "So I went in and put my arms around her saying, 'Now, you know I love you very much.' And then I talked about character and what she did that was wrong, and she listened—never taking her eyes from my face. I began congratulating myself—boy, you are really getting through. She'll remember this when she's 40.

"I talked for 20 minutes. She was spellbound. We were practically nose to nose. As I paused, searching for the clincher, she asked, 'Mommy, how many teeth do you have?'"

There's a message here, of course. The person who needs to recognize it in this type of story is frequently us. However, the humor fades when a raise is lost, a key employee quits, or a sale goes to a competitor. Communication is always a team effort between speaker and listener.

The second basic is that *communication is separate from information.*

Communication is an *act.* Information is the *content.* The medium is *not* the message, and how a message is expressed should not be confused with the content itself. They are two separate components.

The third basic is that *communication is non-repeatable.*

There is never a chance for an identical second exchange after the first attempt. Even with content that is locked in, such as writing or video, readers or viewers change from day to day, from week to week, and are no longer the same people they were when the first exposure occurred. You can never exactly recreate a communication event.

There is also the added factor of the miscues in a first trial affecting the encore. A good example is the classic "Unveiling the New Dress" scene:

From the bedroom, the husband hears, "Close your eyes, hon, I want to show you something I picked up today."

If he's not thinking, the husband says, "Okay." If he is alert, he puts down his tablet, mumbles a short prayer, and replies, "I'm ready!"

The rustle down the hall is punctuated by a fashion runway swirl as the wife asks the hopefully dazzled husband, "How do you like it?"

Frozen in fear, after a short, controlled pause, he states with hopeful enthusiasm, "I really like it!"

"You don't like it! I can tell."

"No, listen, it's really a dynamite dress."

"You hate it, Harold. Any time you say 'really,' I know you're not being truthful."

"Look, what do you want me to say, 'I worship the dress'?" he replies with a rising voice. "I *like* it. I wish we had been married in it. If there was another in the store in a smaller size, I would buy it for my mother. What more do you want, a notarized oath?"

"You don't have to get sarcastic, Harold. You don't like the dress and that's all there is to it. You're never satisfied with anything I do. And speaking of your mother and a smaller size..."

"Stop! Dear, go back in the room and come out again. I *do* like the dress and I'll say whatever you want me to say."

Poor Harold. He might wish he could get another shot at commenting on his wife's new dress. But it is not possible. That's because communication is not repeatable. Next time he'll act ecstatic just to protect himself. If he fumbles that opportunity, he won't get another chance then either.

The fourth communications basic is that *you need to consider the total message whenever you speak.*

People who write about NVC often promote the idea that we are continually communicating "hidden nonverbal messages" that disagree with our verbal messages. This idea may sell a lot of books and seminars, but it just isn't true.

Catchphrases like "What is your body *really* saying?" and "Are you missing the opportunities on those lonely business trips?" merely titillate us. In general, there are very few discrepancies between the overall communications message and NVC. Most people just aren't good enough actors and actresses to carry it off.

As an exercise in college public speaking classes, I would have students give a two–minute talk in which all their gestures and movements had to conflict with what they were saying—what we called "cross talks." For example, they might stomp in, slam their books to the floor, and scream in agony, "I'm glad to be here!"

I limited these talks to two minutes because it takes a great deal of practice to choreograph the movements to each phrase and make them disagree with each other. It is really hard to do. And it is equally hard to have all these so-called hidden messages when you communicate. What happens instead is that you find that all the signs, both verbal and non-verbal, agree with and support each other.

There is a danger in taking a single NVC sign out of context. I discovered this quite by accident when I made a call on one of my regular customers, a utility executive. I naturally had tried to observe his mannerisms for any useful nonverbal information, and he had one habit that drove me to distraction. Whenever I presented an idea to him, either one on one or in a presentation, he always listened with his hand covering his mouth. All the typical NVC literature states that this is a strong sign of disapproval or disagreement.

One day while we were having a casual discussion about a communications column I wrote for a local business periodical, he asked me if I "used" NVC on him, and if I had noticed anything unusual.

"You know, Ken," he said, "I hope I haven't given the wrong impression when I listen to you fellows. Have you noticed anything unusual about me when I listen?"

Sensing I should dig more, I said, "No, Bob. Why would you ask?"

"I read a book that told me I shouldn't put my hand over my mouth when I'm listening. Have you noticed I do this?"

"I've seen it, Bob, but I wasn't sure what it meant," I said. It *had* been bothering me, but I wasn't about to let *him* know that.

He continued, "As you can see, my face is deeply lined. I was riding the bus one day, and just happened to be sitting in a seat where that large convex mirror by the rear door shot my reflection right back at me. I glanced up and saw my face looking grotesque and distorted, glaring back with an enormous frown. The lines on my face made me look terribly negative. It left such an impression on me that I decided to be certain I didn't accidentally make someone think I was angry or unhappy when I was really just listening. Now I always cover my mouth when I listen so that I won't turn the other person off."

That little confession made me breathe a sigh of sales relief. It also taught me a valuable lesson, and unlike most valuable lessons, it came relatively cheap:

No single NVC sign can be read accurately out of the context of the entire communication event.

You need to observe multiple signs. And when they agree, *then* and only then do you have a reliable signal concerning the other person.

To summarize...Nonverbal communication consists of three steps: reading, evaluating, and controlling body signals. Accurate and timely reading of nonverbal information is necessary because of the non-repeatability of the communication process. There is no second chance. Evaluation is necessary to separate information from expression and to better identify the total message. And finally, controlling NVC is necessary because communication is an active process, whether people are listening or speaking.

Getting a "Correlated Read" using NVC checklists

To make it NVC skills easier to learn and use, I have written this book to be efficient and practical in its presentation of ideas. Special emphasis is given to "checklists" of nonverbal signals to help you observe and apply them in social situations, and thereby generate an accurate and reliable read on what is going on beyond the words. Up to now there has been no structured approach to NVC, much less to NVC in business. Yet NVC can play a major role in improving your business image and increasing your chances of success.

EXAMPLE: Winning with NVC—JOE B.

Joe B. is a prime example of how people can be winners with NVC. Before his recent retirement, Joe was one of the foremost architects in a large Midwestern city. Extremely talented, he was known as a super salesman who always won competitive bids. This success was especially remarkable in view of the way organizations select architects.

When a company decides to go out for bids, it typically schedules marathon sessions during which any qualified architect, solicited or otherwise, is allowed to present ideas. On the appointed day the architects assemble outside the conference room like a bevy of shot-putters, flexing their muscles and trying to psych out their opponents. They sit with their drawings rolled up under their arms and nervously wait their turn.

Joe's success was so legendary that when he merely walked into the waiting area, half the architects immediately got up and left without presenting. Joe was an exceptional architect, but he was not that far ahead of his rivals in technical skills. What gave Joe the edge was his superiority in communications skills. He was so superior, in fact, that his competitors began to assume he would win.

In a long conversation with Joe one sunny afternoon, I asked him about his secret. He had a very simple method. "When I go into the room," he said, "I look for two people. The first is the Star, the big boss. He or she is the key decision maker. I make certain I sell to that person and get a commitment. I also look for the Heel. This is the negative person, the one who will make trouble for me when I present and when I'm out of the room. I make sure I put this person in his or her place, and draw out any criticisms so I can respond to them before I leave."

"It all sounds simple enough," I commented, eager for some juicy tips, "but how do you figure out who is the Heel or Star?"

Giving the answer I feared, he responded, "Oh, you can just tell."

Therein lies the excitement of NVC—and the frustration. NVC can increase your chances of business success, but only if you have a systematic technique for learning its vocabulary and applying it in business. Otherwise, you have to "just tell."

The Checklist Approach

The NVC checklists in the first three chapters of this book will give you a framework for learning the vocabulary you need. The three NVC checklists follow the standard pattern of observation: where you put your body, its appearance and what you put around it, and what you do with it once it is there. The remaining chapters will help you gain fluency.

1. Body Position and Status
   Territorial space
   Height might
   Tread spread
   Size prize
   Seating dynamics
   Office etiquette

2. Indicators
   Personal
   Shared
   Public

3. Body Movement
    Center
    Head
    Posture
    Hands
    Legs

With practice, you will be able to make these NVC scans automatically, taking only a few moments to size up a new person or situation. The time is always available, even if you are speaking. Scientists estimate the speed of conversational thought is about 750 words per minute, yet average speech is only about 150 words per minute. This leaves you with 80 percent of your mental capacity to do other things. Frequently, you may daydream or plan your next response with this time. What you ought to do is become a much better "listener" with your eyes.

NVC in Business

You may be curious about how much information you will gain if your eyes do become better listeners. In a classic study that is often misquoted, Albert Mehrabian conducted a series of tests to determine how much body, voice, and words contributed to the communication of *attitudes*. This is an often-applied to communication in general.

So how much do each of these three components contribute in the communication of attitudes—how I feel about me, about you, or about your ideas? Take a moment to fill in your estimates of the percentages. (Remember, the percentages should reflect the communication of *attitudes*, not ideas.)

Body   %
Voice   %
Words   %
TOTAL 100 %

The results of Mehrabian's research were body, 55 percent; voice, 38 percent; and words, 7 percent.

The percentages are, of course, highly dependent on the situation measured. When it is a factual discussion, then clearly words will be the dominant channel for the message. But if there is also an emotional component, then the percentages will change.

In asking my audiences this question over the decades, I would generally get the following numbers: body, 60 percent; voice, 30 percent; and words, 10 percent. That's probably a pretty good rule-of-thumb. The learning point is, our attitudes are often communicated silently. This is the message that most people miss.

If you don't agree with these percentages—if you believe that words are far more important in communicating attitudes— you can do a little research on your own. Try this experiment when you come home from work tomorrow:

As you walk in, tell your loved ones that you do, indeed, love them. Run over to them, shake your fist, and sweetly say, "I love you!" Then walk away snarling, with a horrible grimace on your face, while you clench and unclench your fists.

If words are truly more important than gestures, your loved ones will come over to you with outstretched arms and sweetly respond, "Why, thank you, honey. What a nice surprise. We love you too."

If you survived that experiment, you can follow up with a test on words versus tone of voice. When you come home from work two days later, wait for your loved one to ask, "How was your day, dear?" Then walk over, maintaining as pleasant an expression as possible, arms outstretched for a hug, and scream in a loud voice, "I had just a *wonderful* day!" with as much sarcasm as you can muster.

Once again, if the response is anything other than "That's nice, dear," then voice is also more important than words.

Your experiments will probably need to stop here if you don't want your loved ones to develop a nervous tic when you arrive home. If the responses were calm and oriented solely to your words, you can forget this book. You've somehow landed Mr. Spock from *Star Trek*.

President Franklin Roosevelt was particularly aware of NVC. Standing in a boring receiving line one evening, he decided to have a little fun. As each guest came up and said, "Good evening, Mr. President, how are you, sir?" he responded warmly with a pleasant smile, "Fine, thank you, I just murdered my mother-in-law." Not one person going through the receiving line reacted to his comment. It is doubtful people even heard it. That's the power of nonverbals.

OK...you are now ready to flex your communications muscles at the office. As you walk down the hall tomorrow, try an FDR. When you are asked, "Howya doin'?" smile and cheerfully bubble, "Pretty bad, and you?" Keep count of how many of your fellow workers even hear your words. If *anybody* hears them, he or she is unusually attentive. Most of those you meet will be paying attention only to your nonverbals.

Obviously, words are important and necessary for conveying *ideas* or detailed information. If that weren't true, this book would have to be a video. (Not a bad idea!) In general, your body is the best indicator of *purpose,* and your voice is the best indicator of *importance.*

NVC and Success

NVC has an important impact on all of us. Every President since John F. Kennedy has been tutored in NVC. These politicians realized the tremendous effect of NVC on people's perception of a candidate and on their voting decisions. Your NVC can drastically affect the decisions of your voters—those people in authority who hold your career in their hands.

The animal kingdom, dealing with its human masters, is much more successful than most of us are in using NVC. Even the youngest members are quite adept at seeing into us. If you have ever trained a puppy, you have seen an advanced NVC-reading organism at work.

When you train a puppy, sooner or later you find a "mistake of the second kind" (solid). As you're kneeling there in resigned disgust, your sweet canine bumbles by. You call it, using your kindest, sweetest doggy voice. "Here, Thorndyke! Come here, sweet puppykins. Your faithful and kind owner wants to pet your lovable doggy hide."

Does Thorndyke come? Of course not! He knows full well that he's in deep trouble. You're going to slam his nose in what he did, and banish him to the cold, lonely backyard. He knows because he can read your NVC even though you are trying to appear as kind and nice as possible. You even reinforced his feelings by carrying the paper in your hand.

The first recorded NVC professional was not even human. He was a wizard by the name of Clever Hans who could perform *any* mathematical computation at all. Hans was a horse who lived in Germany in the early 1900s, touring the countryside and giving sellout performances at each stop. He would answer any question from the audience that could be represented by the tapping of a hoof. For a year and a half, audiences were baffled, swearing that there had to be a trick. The show conditions got tougher and tougher, but Hans never missed a question.

Then, after 18 months of success, Hans flopped for the first time. He missed a question that was asked by someone out of his line of sight and kept secret from his trainer. Clever Hans' hoof tapped right past the correct answer. For the first time in his career, Clever Hans was no longer clever.

The reason turned out to be simple. Somehow, Hans had figured out that if he stopped tapping his hoof at a certain point, he would get a reward. Hans was nothing more than a psychologist's rat responding to a stimulus. The stimulus Hans responded to was the tension in his trainer! He found that if he stopped tapping just as the tension eased—that is, just when he had tapped out the answer—he was rewarded. When the question was given to him from someone out of his sight, and kept secret from the trainer, there was no tension to "read."

Hans made his career from NVC, and so have many others in various ways, like Joe B. You too have the capability—if you just take the time to learn the vocabulary of NVC—to improve your business image by bettering your communication skills.

For the first time in your life, you will have the knowledge to interpret some of the massive nonverbal data that used to be summarily shunted to the brain's round file. It is time you added the title Nonverbal Communicator to your business credentials.

CHAPTER 2

Relative Body Location Scan

OUR LANGUAGE RECOGNIZES THE IMPORTANCE of NVC with common body–oriented phrases as:

Cold shoulder
Face up to it
Shake it off
Chin up
Get it off your chest
Grit your teeth
Stiff upper lip
Shoulder a burden
At arm's length
Glad-hander

These phrases are almost more than we can swallow. You've got to hand it to me, though, the ones I dug up are real eye-openers. I can keep them coming hand over fist, until your knees buckle. But don't let your spirits droop. I promise to quit slinging these out before you turn your back in disgust.

The term *body language*, popularized by Julius Fast in his book of the same name, refers to the portion of NVC relating solely to physical communication, excluding voice.

Body language is actually the study of three concepts: proxemics, indicators, and kinesics. *Proxemics* (derived from the Greek word meaning, "to approach") covers the analysis of body location. *Indicators,* a sociological term, refers to the objects we gather around us. *Kinesics* is the study of physical movements.

In coming chapters you will not only examine these three areas, but you will also cover vocal traits, environment, and image as key nonverbal signals of attitude. This chapter introduces the checklist for evaluating body position and status:

Territorial Space
Height Might
Tread Spread
Size Prize
Seating Dynamics
Office Etiquette

Territorial Space

The first questions you should ask yourself in any business situation is, "Where are people located and why are they there?" The distance we maintain with others is related to our feelings toward them, and indicates something about our relationships. This distance is called *territorial space.* There are four basic zones of territorial space: intimate, personal, social, and public.

Intimate Space

Intimate space includes distances up to about one and one-half feet. It is used for such activities as lovemaking, comforting, protecting, or family greetings. It is also used for wrestling, basketball, sitting in movie theaters, and standing in elevators or on crowded street corners.

Intimate space is usually reserved for people who have the right to be that close to us. Such familiarity and relaxation of normal distance preferences most often require time and a deepening of relationships. Sometimes this is not always possible, as in an elevator, where closeness to strangers makes most of us feel uncomfortable.

The importance of maintaining my own intimate space was brought home to me one afternoon. A salesman and I were having a casual conversation about the poor economy when I began to get nervous. The salesman kept shifting closer to me as we talked, stopping at a distance of a foot, which put our faces all of nine inches apart. I decided to try a little experiment, partly out of interest and mostly out of self-preservation.

Fortunately, we were at his desk, out in the middle of a large room, so I had plenty of space to work with. As we talked, I slowly backed around the desk, leaning forward all the while, keeping my face somewhat close to his. Then I tried to "wean" him off my face by slowly leaning back and standing upright. Sure enough, as I did that he unconsciously took a step around the desk, got up close again, and I was back in his clutches. I performed the maneuver again, so that I was now on the opposite side of the desk from where we started, but the results were the same. I was trapped!

Deciding it was time for more serious measures, I had a flash of brilliance, I sat on the desk so I could stick my knees out between us. But he moved to stand between my legs. At this point, I was desperate. In a last-ditch effort, I leaned back on my hands away from him as I sat. He then leaned forward until I yelled, "Stop! Is give up! I give up! You win!"

"What do you mean?" was the quizzical, unmoving reply.

"Don't move a muscle, Mike," I then I put my thumb on my nose, and touched his nose with the little finger of the same hand. He was literally a hand's breadth away from me, leaning over the desk.

"You're just too damn close for my personal comfort! You are only *that* far away from my face," I said, showing him my outstretched hand. "My *wife* and I don't even converse at this distance!"

"Well, that's your problem, Cooper!" he returned, stomping off in a huff.

Later Mike came back to me and mentioned that several customers he had asked about it felt as I did. You can't use intimate space unless you have earned the right to be there.

In fact, police purposely use space invasion as an interrogation tactic. One of my students, a county police officer, talked about using this approach in questioning suspects. Leaning forward, he would draw his chair up to the seated suspect until his knee touched the chair between the suspect's knees. He and the other officers would trade off the questioning stints, never letting the suspect regain his territorial space. As the officer put it, "Who needs rubber hoses when I can crowd them as long as I like?"

Personal Space

Personal space includes distances of one and one-half feet to four feet. Personal distance is normally maintained between two friends in conversation—for example, at a small lunchroom table. Office workers standing around the water cooler will often maintain this distance, as will people at a cocktail party who know each other. Reduce the distance to intimate space, and your acquaintance will become very uncomfortable, most likely moving away to restore the personal space.

One of the oddities of TV, that is not readily apparent to the viewer, is that actors often have to talk almost nose to nose in a close-up shot.

A humorous example is the "medicinal elixir" commercial where a pleasant young couple stands against a black backdrop and the husband says something like, "This is my wife and I love her. Because she knows she's important, she takes Killital to maintain our love."

The ridiculous part of this commercial is that the man and woman are right on top of each other. He is breathing hotly on her forehead and she is craning her neck to smile and look up to him with love. Real people, no matter how intimate, don't talk to each other three inches apart. Even at rip-roaring drunken brawls, at least personal distance is maintained (for conversation, naturally).

Social Space

Social space is approximately four to seven feet. Phrases such as "stand back so I can see you" and "keep him at arm's length" reflect our need for social space.

In business, the prime protector of social space is the desk. It automatically puts the heads of the people seated on either side about seven feet apart. The same goes for a conference table, dining table, or counter in a store. That is why they are the size they are.

Studies of trends in office furniture have shown that status-conscious top executives are getting rid of their desks, files, and drawers, figuring they are above all that. But they are still replacing their desks with tables of approximately the same size, in order to maintain control of the social space around their chair.

Strangers thrown together at a party will initially form circles at social space. For example, at social gatherings I often try to determine who already knows whom and who just met by observing how far apart people are standing.

Recently I had a half-hour discussion with a man who knew I was an NVC consultant. He spent the time arguing that NVC is B.S. and a complete waste of time. I was happy to let him ramble, because as we were talking I moved closer and then farther away. He was unconsciously shifting his position to maintain his own comfortable social space.

In the course of the conversation, we meandered up and down a hall and in and out of two offices, ending up where the hall met the office areas. After he finished one particularly long tirade, I said, "Look, I'll buy what you said about NVC if you can answer one simple question for me."

"Sure," he sneered. "What is it?"

"Tell me," I returned, "why have you and I been in and out of a hall and two offices at least twice in the past half-hour if personal space wasn't important to you?"

He stared at me for a moment and stomped off. I may not have gained a convert, but I won an argument—nonverbally.

Public Space

Public space, usually ten feet or more, is reserved for strangers whom we don't care to notice or interact with. People waiting in the lobby for an elevator will mill about at this distance. Even on a busy street corner people will try to maintain this space. Watch public places such as lobbies, transportation terminals, reception areas, or museums for how strangers maintain public space.

The importance of public space was illustrated by a formal experiment performed at a college library. A graduate assistant went to the library when it was relatively empty and purposely sat at an occupied table. Responses varied from complete indifference, to dirty looks, to disgusted stares. Yet in 80 trials, only one person asked the grad student to move. The assistant finally asked to be replaced in the experiment because the subjects in the library made her feel so guilty for intruding.

Controlling Territories

There is a wealth of information to be gained from observing how attendees mill about before a meeting or "shoot the breeze" around

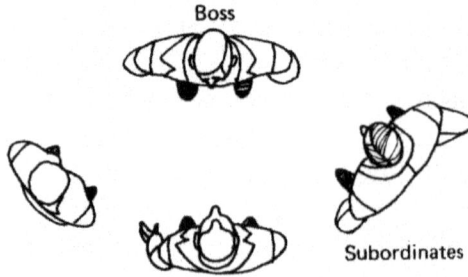

Figure 2–1. Standing positions.

the cooler. For example, it is easy to determine which person is the leader in a group.

When a superior is talking with a number of subordinates, the configuration often takes on a "choir effect," as shown in Figure 2–1. The leader, at the top of the diagram, is given more space. The others are facing the leader in a semicircle. The "choir" will usually stand attentively, rarely turning to leave unless someone else arrives to fill the gap.

In a leaderless group, it is apparent who is "in" or "out" by their physical position. In Figure 2–2 the person on the lower left has walked up to a conversation and been recognized but not admitted to the group. Notice how the two people on either side of the newcomer have created a small gap, but not enough to give the newcomer equal space. All of us have been in this predicament at one time or another and often walk away with no small feeling of rejection.

The territorial space characteristics of an individual's office or workspace are indicative of its owner. An executive may want to crowd visitors to his or her office by placing the desk about a third of

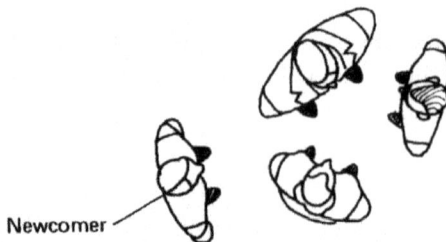

Figure 2–2. Unwelcome newcomer.

the way between the door and the back wall. This way, the executive has ample space to lean away from the desk, put feet up, or swivel. The visitor has little space, which connotes less importance or dominance.

One client of mine laid out his office in this manner. He placed a large tree on the visitor's side, so that there was just enough room between the desk, tree, and wall for a chair. I could not cross my legs in the chair, much less be comfortable. Of course, my client always apologized for the size of the office, but I've heard he has had the opportunity to move to a bigger one and has refused several times.

The amount of available space can also affect the success of a meeting. I always avoid using a small classroom in my training sessions, because the audience is much more argumentative and harder to control. The same holds true for a business meeting. If there is not enough personal space for the participants, the meeting has a much smaller chance for success as time passes.

We often use objects to mark our territorial space, much as a dog "anoints" a new backyard to indicate its territory. People sitting on a bus or plane will fill the other seat with their belongings to "claim" the space.

On the *Tonight Show*, actress Angie Dickinson once mentioned that she prefers to read during a flight rather than talk to other passengers. So when the flight was not full, she always put her carry-on luggage and accessories in the seat next to her until right before departure to discourage anyone from sitting there.

Walls can also be used to define territorial space. Members of a department will fill the walls within their boundaries with pictures, contest posters, or other paraphernalia to indicate the department's physical territory.

Sometimes, we have to claim our territory personally. At a "husbands and wives too" office party, an executive I know was having an animated conversation with his young secretary. They were sitting on the couch and she was touching his arm as they talked, holding his eyes with a steady gaze. Suddenly his wife came over, sat down beside him, smoothed his collar, and listened without saying a word. The move was a show of possession, reminding the secretary of the wife's "territory." The message was not lost on the secretary, because the conversation ended soon afterwards and was not resumed that evening.

Men use the same sort of maneuver at social gatherings to demonstrate relationships with their wives or women friends. A man comes up to a woman and casually slips an arm around her waist. In effect, he is saying to the other man, "She's mine, remember?"

Territorial space can be manipulated to gain control, as in the police interrogation example described earlier. Intruding on people's space is one of the most common forms of domination in business. Some people can make us feel like a rabbit at the wolves' convention by talking close to us, as Mike did. The effect can be intensified by offensive personal habits.

If you have a tough meeting coming up, schedule it in a small conference room and anticipate it with a big, garlic lunch. Rope-sized cigars made from buffalo chips are another executive weapon in the discomfort race. Chest poking (the female version is arm punching), nudging (remember Monty Python's "Nudge, Nudge" sketch?), and backslapping are further insults to our sense of space. After 20 minutes of one of the above, most of us are ready to agree to almost anything.

If you want to hold an efficient, spirited meeting, keep the space tight. This can help shorten the duration better than any schedule. Small spaces also intensify conflict. In making recommendations to management negotiators at a large chemical plant, I suggested that they meet with the union local in a "cozy" little conference room. This was to take advantage of the well-known antagonism between the young union president and an old-line vice-president. Although the negotiating sessions were prolonged, the union's inability to present a united front was beneficial to the company.

If you wish to reduce conflict in a session, provide more space. Spread everyone out around a large table in a spacious room. Make them totally comfortable.

In general, become aware of others' needs for territorial space. By moving closer or farther away during a conversation, see if you can determine the space your business associates and acquaintances prefer, and then use that distance.

As you grow more familiar with the uses of territorial space, you will be able to continue conversations others are trying to break off by keeping within conversational distance. You will learn to stay farther away from people who are trying to control you and to get closer to those you wish to leverage. You will discover that territorial space is both an indicator and a tool in effective NVC.

Height Might

Height has long been associated with the desirable, with success. Up is good and down is bad. Our language is full of phrases such as: look up to him, raised to the peerage, put on a pedestal, on top of the world, rise to the occasion, and high and mighty. No self-respecting god would ever be caught down low, in Death Valley or the Bonneville Salt Flats. They live in places like Mt. Olympus and Valhalla.

Height is also a symbol of power and superiority. Royalty sits high up on a throne. The winner stands on the top Olympic platform step. A judge's courtroom bench is always elevated. Victorious football players put the coaches on their shoulders and carry them off the field.

You even see it in courtroom dramas, like the old classic *Perry Mason*. Raymond Burr never went up to the judge's bench to argue an objection. He did it from afar. How could he appear in control if he stood there like a youngster filching cookies off the counter? That was okay for an opponent like Hamilton Burger, but not for our Perry!

Lack of height has always been a negative sign. We can fall short of a goal, think small, be shortsighted, or look down on someone.

Being lower can also be a sign of servility. In ancient times, vanquished soldiers were forced to pass under a chest-high arch of spears in front of the conquering general. Anyone who refused to bow down was allowed to wear a spear home, buried in his chest. Even today we don't like anyone to "lord it over us."

Figure 2–3. Height might.

(Copyright ©1977 King Features Syndicate Inc.)

We consistently favor people with a height advantage, ala Figure 2–3. For example, taller presidential candidates tend to win more often. (Two presidential winners who were shorter than their opponents were Richard Nixon at 5'11-1/2" over a 6' 1" George McGovern, and Jimmy Carter at 5'9-1/2" "over" a 6' 1" Gerald Ford. Note that both were in the era of TV campaigning, where height differences are purposely made neutral.)

Business also rewards height. A 1972 study of University of Pittsburgh graduates showed that those in the 6'2" to 6'4" range received twelve percent higher starting salaries than their fellow graduates, independent of any other factors.

The dominance of height in terms of relative eye level is no secret to today's business executive. For example, everyone knows the importance of standing up to address a meeting in order to gain control.

Many executives choose their office furniture so they can dominate visitors. They sit on large, high-backed, elevated desk chairs while offering their visitors low-slung lounge chairs that are almost impossible to get out of, much less sit up in.

You can't saw the legs off of someone who is taller than you or modify their office furniture in secret, but there are ways to minimize a height disadvantage. As pointed out in the section on territorial space, distance is a good counteragent for height dominance. A 6'4" executive who is overwhelming up close is almost completely neutralized at public distances. Sitting at opposite ends of the table, talking from the door of his office, or getting up and moving while you talk will all help you stay even.

A 5'9" IBM sales training manager claimed that he could minimize height might in tough sales calls on any tall executives. Just when the customer was bearing down the hardest, perhaps leaning over the desk and slamming points home, the manager would get up and walk over to a window and begin gazing out thoughtfully. He would continue the conversation with, "Now, you've made several good points here. Let me see if I understand them."

As he restated the customer's position, occasionally glancing back toward the desk, the customer would often calm down and begin to agree or amplify. Sometimes the customer would even follow him to the window. Then the conversation would continue more rationally as both men pondered the outdoors. Only when the meeting was back on an even basis would the manager return to his chair, successful in escaping a tough situation.

Another way to minimize height differences is to carefully control the location of any conversation or meeting. Like the spider, you should conduct business safely in your web—your office. Adjust the height of your desk chair if needed. Find visitors' chairs that are soft and comfortable, but not so low as to be obvious. Some executives have even had hidden platforms constructed behind their desks.

Make your office or workspace the one place where you can be in control. Save important conversations for times when you can invite your boss in.

When you can't arrange a conversation in your office, at least hold it outside of the other person's office. Talk over lunch if you must. It is almost impossible for an associate to be domineering when special sauce is running out the corner of their mouth or when they are munching a hard luncheon roll with crumbs bouncing from plate to lap. In addition, being in public limits the tactics the other person can use.

Other places where height advantage is relatively meaningless are in a car or airplane, in a bar or lounge with deep chairs, or in a crowd.

Being outnumbered also tends to neutralize height might. One of my former managers used to pack subordinates into his small office for weekly team meetings. Just for fun, I made a point of coming in last when all the chairs were taken. The only spot left was a heater module, which was about desk high and somewhat behind the manager's chair. When I sat on it I was head and shoulders above him and to his rear. The first few meetings I did this he was slightly uneasy but accepted my excuse about no place to sit. The third meeting he *ordered* me to get a chair.

This still wasn't acceptable, because he continued to be surrounded. Even if he had stood up, his height dominance would have affected only the people he was facing. He could not address the people at his sides without twisting around. This dynamic of groups can help you make up in numbers what you may lack in physical positioning.

A final approach to minimizing height advantage is to act more assertively. An administrator in a sales office felt he was being treated unfairly, but he knew he would be lost if he went in to talk with the office manager. The manager was a tall man and a smooth, persuasive talker. Deciding on an aggressive approach, the administrator worked himself into a suitable "mad" and stormed into the office. He strode up to the manager's desk and began telling him what was wrong, pounding the desk to emphasize his points. This continued for a few minutes until the manager slipped in during a pause and said, "Jack, Jack! Sit down and we'll talk about it."

Jack responded with, "I can't sit down, I'm too upset!" and continued to talk. The manager finally stood up, at which point Jack abruptly said, "I'm sorry I've gotten so worked up. We'll have to talk about it when I get myself calmed down," and walked out to lunch. The story ended happily when the problem was later resolved, which Jack insists was due solely to his aggressive tactics.

If you are among those of us who won't be getting that twelve percent higher starting salary, you now have several techniques to use against those who will. Being "one up" is often little more than being physically up, a situation you can handle by using the information in this chapter to "stand tall" with others.

Tread Spread

A variation on height dominance, and the third item on the body position and status scanning checklist, is *walking position.*

Like being "on top," being a "front-runner" is an indicator of status and power. (Why else do we speed up when an old VW tries to pass?) In a military inspection, the highest-ranking reviewing officer always walks in front. In a procession of royalty, the monarch is always at the head.

I have never seen a picture of former President Ford and former Secretary Kissinger when Kissinger was not sensitive enough to remain in the background. Some cultures require people of lower status to walk at least one step behind their superiors.

It's even politically important. State department officials closely examine all photos of dignitaries from "restricted" countries such as Russia and China. In pictures of a group walking, power or status is shown by how near the front of the pack an individual is.

Can you imagine the CEO of your organization walking down the hall leaning over your boss's shoulder to talk? Ridiculous. Yet the chances are you've seen a subordinate of the CEO walking in that position.

One of my students, a bank vice-president, remarked, "So that's why I always end up walking through the bank sideways like a sand crab, talking to one of my people. I've even mentioned it to a few of them, but we still end up this way, with them behind me."

Observe walking position in meeting a new group, or sitting in the lobby of a new client. I used to watch groups of my customers come out of the elevator, walk up to the reception desk, then arrange themselves around the sign-in counter. The boss would usually lead the way. In the instances where the boss trailed, the others would wait for their manager to do the talking and to sign in first.

If one person defers and lets another go ahead, that is another indicator of higher status. An underling does not usually defer to the boss. The boss goes ahead as a matter of course. The subordinate never had the privilege of being ahead in the first place!

I'm frequently asked, "What about a man who opens the door for a woman? What does that mean?" This one is a bit more complex. With some men, this is merely a courtesy out of habit or from upbringing. Some women have no problem with it. Some are offended by it.

In a *business* setting, opening a door for someone is usually an indicator of relative status. Ignoring the differences in gender, wouldn't you be nervous if, during a long stroll through your office building, your boss carefully opened every door for you? You might think, "I've got to stop letting this happen. I'm looking lazy or insensitive!" You end up rushing to the next door to usher your boss in first. Your manager isn't supposed to be serving *you*.

So it's time to step out and become a front-runner. One of the hardest things to do is to take initiative. Foursomes bumble at the restaurant desk, indecisive about which couple should ask for the reservations. If we are between two others walking along the street and are forced to crowd down to two wide because of people coming the other way, we are the ones who step into the evasive tap dance trying to save our shins as we fall behind. We are part of that pack milling around the reception desk or hesitating self-consciously at a doorway.

In your office, think about no longer walking behind your bosses. Stay even, or walk in front of them occasionally. Women, open the door for men, man-style and usher people through, as the opportunity arises. These little changes in walking position can go a long way in building confidence and showing your power.

Size Prize

Another variation on height might is size prize, or physical bulk. Our society idolizes size. Bigger is usually considered to be better.

The respect and love of bigness is *everywhere*. Kids watch a Saturday morning cereal commercial that praises the stuff solely for its size. A group of kids in a beat-up wooden hideout sing, "Honeycrumb's big. Big, BIg, BIG! Got a big bite. Right, RIGht, RIGHT! Honeycrumb's a big mouthful, it tastes just right!" Who cares if it's nutritional or if it tastes like outdoor rug glue, as long as it totally fills up your mouth?

Many consumer products focus on bigness. If your soap isn't selling, bring it out in a new, larger container. The words "big" and "large" have become so overworked that companies have come up with "family size" and "industrial size" just to announce even more bigness. After all, where else but in America could a fast-food franchise succeed on the strength of a product named the Whopper?

Movies also have to be big. Papers are filled with ads such as:

See *Tidal Jaws: The Towering Earthquake Adventure, 1932.* With a cast of billions. See the destruction of the entire earth in Sound-abound. Feel, breathe the panoramic majesty of massive death. Thrill to the biggest galaxy of stars since the Crab Nebula in a glut of cameo roles. Watch, as Ralph, the mechanical earth, a 100 percent scale model, self-destructs, bringing the entire studio down with it.

Even our activities have to be big. "This is the biggest thing that ever happened to this town." A perennially popular book is a collection of world records on "the most." Heavyweights are the only boxers many general sports fans follow. Even the most ardent collegiate football fan probably has no idea that there is a lightweight collegiate football league in the Northeast.

Physical bulk is an enormous advantage in today's business world. Several years ago, my office had a chance to interview the graduating captain of Notre Dame's football team. Even though he was a fine offensive tackle, he felt he would have a hard time making it in the pros, so he was interviewing for a position through the college placement office. He was a giant—your average, run-of-the-mill Notre Dame offensive lineman. This was no stereotypical dumb jock. He owned a high grade point average and had excellent leadership qualities. But what do you think the comments from management were?

"Did you see that guy we had in here today? He could have bent my arm with one hand and tossed me through the window with a flick of the wrist! And he's even qualified."

"Man, if we land that hulk, we'll have a real superstar on our hands."

"He can't miss. Can you imagine letting him call on (customer name deleted)? He'd eat that little pipsqueak alive."

To the football player's credit, he turned down a very lucrative offer, one, I suspect, higher than any other trainee received. For some reason, everyone in the office acted as if we still carry clubs. Evidently we do, only they are psychological clubs.

Remember the University of Texas football slogan of the late 1960s? "If you've got it, flaunt it!" If you are blessed with physical size (not bloat, you will read about that later), maximize its effect. Maintain closer territorial spaces, dwarf everything you come in contact with. Have a smaller desk and keep the chairs tightly grouped. If you have a large office, jam the furniture into one small area, and decorate the empty space or turn it into an unused "casual setting."

Emphasize your physical bulk. Give iron handshakes, talk loudly, slap backs, and punch shoulders. Tell people you play in an adult hockey league for the physical contact. Rugby is even better. (Every rugby player I ever met thought a minor injury was one where you could at least get up before the game was over. A major injury has never been defined.)

One of my customers was an enormous man who would rather crush your hand than look at you. Though I have a fairly large, powerful hand, I was still on the edge of agony every time I greeted him. I was careful to remove my ring before making any calls on him. He had the habit of pulling his hand back slightly so that my knuckles were in his grasp and my second and fourth fingers were crushed against the unyielding ring. It was impossible to be assertive with this man while nursing a mutilated paw.

Another man in our office let it be known that he had been a heavyweight boxing champion in his youth and used to earn extra money by staying in the ring three rounds with carnival knockout artists. All he had to do at a meeting was to begin to get a little agitated or start pounding the table, and the others would back off. Although there had never been the hint of a disturbance in his business career, he used this veiled threat successfully for years.

If you are small or slight, you can minimize your lack of size by manipulating your environment. Get a massive desk. Use large, high-armed, heavy office chairs that cannot be moved easily and place them slightly away from your desk. Large bookshelves, enormous paintings, giant displays, or charts all serve to minimize size differences between people. Imagine two men standing under the Gateway Arch in St. Louis, one is 6'4" and the other 5'8". Size becomes unimportant because they are both dwarfed by their surroundings.

Don't worry about drawing attention to your size with this approach, particularly if you have a large office. If your office is small, use lighting to help achieve the same effect. Don't use bright ceiling lights. Take out several ceiling bulbs at night if you have to. Keep the room a comfortable brightness, like a family room, and use an attractive desk lamp for working. Bright light brings out the details of size, making a room and everything in it look smaller. Softer lighting minimizes any negative feature, such as a bad paint job or worn furniture. The more ornate and impressive your trappings are, the less your physical bulk will matter. Is it any wonder that the boss Mr. Foofram in the "Hi and Lois" comic strip has a big, fancy office?

The key to overcoming lack of size is to battle the problem subtly. Small statured people in business face a strange double bind. If they are aggressive and successful, they are accused of having a Napoleon complex. They are "overcompensating." Remarks such as, "She's a tiger for such a little girl" and "He's a real bantam rooster" abound. These are negative compliments of the worst kind.

The truly successful person in business must develop a style that does not let the question of size ever become a concern. Even if some of the funds must come from your own pocket, make your office the one place where your personal features are maximized. Don't go in for elevator shoes or a Napoleon personality. Let competence speak for you.

One of the most dynamic people I have ever met also has one of the best corporate styles I have ever seen. He started as the proprietor of a small hardware store and built it into a chain of retail sales and rental stores. After retiring at 32 for two years, he decided to re-enter business and is now vice-president of a large construction firm. If you are familiar with the construction industry, you know it has the biggest collection of hard-nosed, burly brutes in the working world. There is no room for the meek or mild. But this executive has the complete respect and cooperation of everyone who works for him.

He has never heard any of the short-guy put-downs, nor has he heard any Napoleon remarks. He works with overwhelming, inarguable competence. He never has to raise his voice. He never makes rash judgments. Because there is so little doubt about him as a businessman, there is also little doubt about him as a man. True competence, controlled competence, is the only way to escape the stature put-down and double-bind.

One of my evening college students was a department manager in a large retail company, and a former Miss Tall beauty pageant winner. Only 21 years of age, she was the first executive manager ever to reach that level without a college degree. An imposing young woman of 6'4" in height, I asked what her secret was.

"I was very lucky when I was younger," she revealed, "because both my parents were imposing and thought I would be, too. They made a point of making me proud of my size, even during those years growing up when it was hard being taller than everyone. So many of my female friends who are tall slump and act ashamed of their height. They try to minimize it, to act smaller. My folks taught me to stand up straight and be proud of myself."

As an experiment, I included this question on this classes' midterm exam: "How should a tall woman manage her proxemics (body location) for maximum effect?" Four out of six women and all seven men in the class assumed that she should *de*-emphasize her size advantage. The retail manager was the only person who said she should leverage it.

If you are blessed with natural stature and size advantages, don't make the same mistake as the rest of those students. You've got it. Use it!

Seating Dynamics

Ever since Joe and Buck, the first two cavemen with the dawning of intelligence in their eyes, decided that there must be something better than working doubled up on the ground like a duck, people have vied for status through seating position. Joe probably found a flat-sided rock and rolled it over to the cave for Buck to see (which is not easy to do with a flat-sided rock, but then again they were cavemen). One of them, undoubtedly Buck, suddenly had the bright idea of laying it flat side *up*, and in a flash the table was born. The little scene surely ended with an argument over who would get to sit at the narrow end of the rock.

The point is, the locations we choose for sitting are loaded with nonverbal data. Remember the Paris peace talks that ended the Vietnam war? Diplomats spent several *years* trying to determine the seating arrangements for the various delegates. Seating arrangements are no less important in business.

Association Approximation

Certain seating positions are conducive to different types of interaction. By observing those positions, we can begin to draw fairly accurate conclusions about relationships. Figure 2–4 shows four variations in seating dynamics.

Cooperation is best when people are sitting next to each other. When a teacher is tutoring a student or an office worker is showing a replacement how to do a certain job, they usually sit next to each other so both can work from the same document.

Conversation is facilitated when people are sitting at adjacent corners of a table. The company lunchroom is a good place to observe this. (If the table is small, though, conversation may be uncomfortable because of insufficient territorial space. In this case, the two people

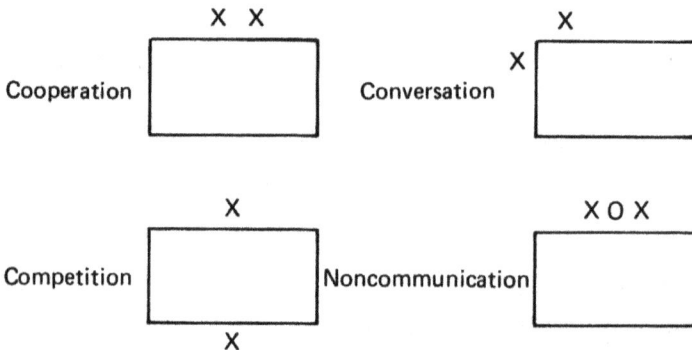

Figure 2–4. Sitting positions.

will sit across from each other.) Conversation requires closeness, but not to the same degree as sharing reading material.

Competitors often confront each other face to face, like Western gunslingers. Opponents in a meeting tend to sit across the table from each other, either at the middle or at each end. This way, each one can "keep an eye on" the other. Their underlings or support personnel frequently choose the seats on either side of their "gunslinger," much like lining up for the showdown at the corral.

If there is to be no fight, the opponents may choose the non-communication position, with someone sitting between them. The more people between them, the harder it is to converse. The effect is similar to trying to talk to a relative at the Thanksgiving table with a hearty eater bobbing up and down between you. You end up leaning back and forth like an antenna in the carwash.

Table Status

You should be familiar with the dominant and subordinate positions around a rectangular business meeting table. The dominant positions are the ends. The middle of the table is a secondary dominant position and is usually used for active defense or for disagreement with the leader on the end. The weakest positions are in between the powers, in the "dead zone" of status.

The first table in Figure 2–5 shows the normal primary and secondary positions of power and opposition around a rectangular table. This arrangement is common in meetings of a committee of equals with an appointed chairperson or in meetings where the chairperson has a higher position.

The second table arrangement is likely when the meeting contains a hierarchy of personnel. I have noticed this pattern frequently in military meetings, where the general sits at the head of the table and those along the side are arranged by rank, with the lowly lieutenants sitting meekly at the far end. This is sometimes called the King Arthur arrangement, in honor of the round table, which supposedly had no status. (Instead, the knights fought to see who could sit closest to King Arthur.)

The third table in Figure 2–5 shows a multiple King Arthur arrangement where multiple executives has grouped minions around them. In this situation, relative status is determined by the number of chairs

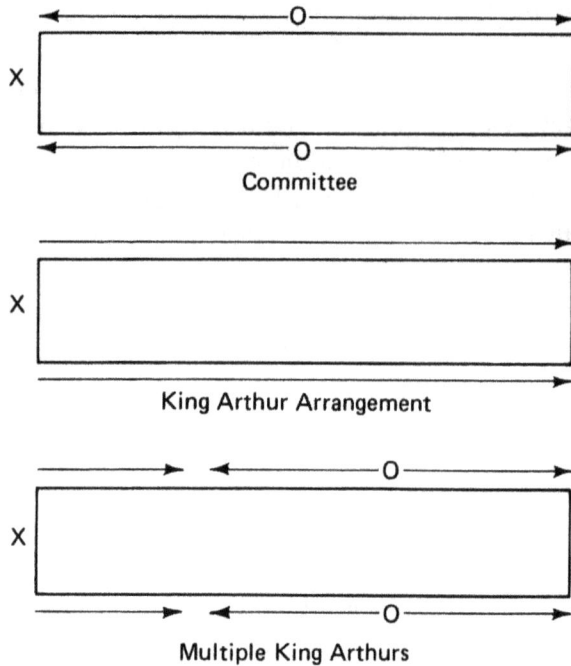

Committee

King Arthur Arrangement

Multiple King Arthurs

Key:

X = Dominant Positions
O = Secondary Dominant Positions
→ = Direction of Decreasing Status

Figure 2–5. Table status.

between a person and his or her King Arthur. See if these observations about seating behavior hold in your organization. You may find that this is one of the primary indicators of power.

Rear Fear

There is a special case of seating dynamics called rear fear, which may date back to the wild, wild West.

"Okay, you cowpokes and gunslingers. What's the one rule to follow when you're sipping your favorite firewater at the Longbranch Saloon? That's right, tenderfoot. Never sit with yer back to the door! You never know when some filthy varmint will come up and plug ya."

Today, many people will first fill the restaurant tables along the wall and may even leave rather than sit in the middle of the dining area. In general, people do not like to sit with their backs to the door because it makes them feel exposed. Less than one percent of the offices I have seen are arranged facing away from the door.

In one case, the office of a principal in a CPA firm, people often sat down in the *occupant's* chair instead of the visitor's chair, which faced the door. Even though the layout of the office was clear, the visitor could not imagine that the principal would sit with his back exposed. Another office arranged "backward" had a beautiful view of St. Louis' Gateway Arch, which the advertising-executive occupant could not bear to miss.

Your relationship to the door is also important in meetings or negotiating sessions. If you wish to feel more secure, try to sit with your back to the wall. If you don't want to overpower others, let them sit facing the door.

Sitting with your back to the door can be very disruptive, because frequent noises from outside may drive your curiosity to the breaking point. Some negotiators use a noise in the hall or interruptions such as a secretary coming in to ask, "Is George Finster Here? There's been a terrible accident," to unsettle their opposites. There may not even be a George Finster, but everyone will go crazy wondering what the "accident" was. Start noticing what is behind you and others, be it a wall or a door, and try to determine how it is affecting everyone's sense of security and comfort.

Zones of Attention

Where we sit can greatly affect our attentiveness at a meeting, presentation, or lecture. In college, I knew many students who forced themselves to sit in the front row because they knew they would learn more there. We have all been in the position of arriving late and having to go to the front of the room for the only available chairs, watched every step of the way by the audience and speaker! Once settled, there we sat, uncomfortably exposed to the probing eyes of the lecturer. Afraid to show our attention lagging, we hung on every word, no matter how dull.

People in this "front and center" position give the most attention to the speaker. Those in the middle section pay the next highest amount of attention and ask questions next most frequently. The middle zone is a good, safe area, with people comfortably surrounded by others. Attention and interaction decrease as the listener sits farther back in the room. The side zones are even less responsive and attentive.

The worst listening area is filled with "balcony Baptists." I once had an elderly neighbor who would sit in the balcony of the local church and sleep. It was a very considerate sleep, though, since he learned to hold his head at an angle that would reflect the chandeliers' light from his glasses into the pulpit. That way, he felt he wasn't insulting the pastor by blatantly sleeping through the sermons. In any meeting room, remember: "If you want them to sleep, sit them deep!"

That said, it's better to arrange the seats a little deeper than wider, once you are beyond the first few rows. Try to keep a depth-to-width ratio of about 3 to 2 before widening the rows. This way, you will keep more people located in a better zone of attention.

Also, don't ignore the territorial space needs of your audience. It's better to have 80 percent of the crowd present, comfortable and attentive, than to have 100 percent of your audience crowded and unruly. (The missing 20 percent will be told you were wonderful anyway, which is better than hearing you and leaving it to chance.)

If you can set up a lecture room, keep the door to your side or back. That way, if there is an interruption, you can control it, resolve it in front of your listeners so they can satisfy their curiosity, and continue without waiting for people to turn around again and settle in their seats.

If you are plagued with latecomers, such as at an after-dinner speech or early morning meeting, arrange the chairs with the door in the rear and leave a chairless area four or five rows in size at the back as a noise buffer zone.

Don't overstock the room with chairs before your audience arrives. People will sit as far back as you let them. Have some chairs stacked ready in the buffer zone at the beginning of the meeting, just in case. But don't put them out. Otherwise you'll have half the audience sitting back there from the start.

If you are attending a meeting, find out ahead of time who else will be there. Arrive early enough to have your choice of seats if possible. Let others have their backs to the door if it suits your purpose. Sit there yourself only when you *choose to*. Find out if you are part of a King Arthur competitive group. Sit close to your King if you can, but perhaps not too close to the head of the meeting, unless he or she is also your King. If you're one of the Kings, determine ahead of time who is in control and what your attitude is toward the leader. Then choose your position accordingly. If you are the leader, you should be picking out your Stars and Heels, like Joe B. did in Chapter 1.

Finally, note the relative positions of the group. Whom can you talk to easily and comfortably with no one else in the way? Who "opposes" you across the table? If the meeting has no formal leader, who has picked the leader's position nonverbally? If you wish to gain control, are you in the proper position for it? If you ask yourself these questions each time you sit down at a meeting, you will be well on your way to using seating dynamics successfully.

Office Etiquette

The moment-enclosed offices are established in any organization, an unwritten procedure develops for entering an office and responding to a visitor. As a salesman, I enjoyed sitting in a reception area and watching the private offices while I waited for a customer. The relative status of the office occupant and the visitor was apparent the moment the visitor stepped up to the door.

For example, someone comes up to an office door, hesitates with a single brief knock, then proceeds in. The occupant looks up and waves the visitor to a chair. Who has the higher status? The visitor is most likely of a slightly lower status or an immediate underling who has a casual relationship with the superior. Why? The two key points in this scene are the pause at the door and the boss's recognition of the subordinate.

If your home is your castle, then your office is your fortress. In general, a subordinate respects this and will pause at the door before entering. In the case above, the pause was almost negligible, connoting a close relationship or status. The longer the visitor waits at the door, the lower the status.

If there is *no* wait—if the visitor strides in without pause—then the visitor has a *higher* status, showing no respect for a subordinate's office.

The response of the office occupant is another indicator of relationships. The faster the occupant stands up, the higher the status of the visitor. In the case above, the occupant didn't stand up, but merely waved the subordinate to a chair. Had it been one of the organization's higher-level executives, the manager would have jumped from the chair!

Treat your office with respect. One of my former bosses had a curious practice that stripped him of all office status. He kept a jar of candy sitting on a table by the door for anyone to take. People popped in and out, no matter what was going on, mumbling, "Just wanted this," "Thanks," or "Excuse me." Everyone had an reason to enter his office at will, uninvited, and people did, disrupting anyone else who was in there with him. He gained no status from his office. As a result, he had to close the door frequently, turning away legitimate visitors. He could have stopped the distractions more effectively (and saved some money) by killing the candy dish!

Start noticing your behavior when you enter any office in your organization. Do you uphold "office etiquette"? Are there subordinates who don't recognize yours? If you are vying for promotion with one of your contemporaries, who has a more casual relationship with your boss, whom does your boss respect more?

If you visit other offices as a consultant, auditor, or internal adviser, can you determine the relative status of people before you meet them and learn their names? Can you use the behavior at the door to figure out the relative status of a newcomer who's been invited to sit in on an office meeting? These are all questions office etiquette can help answer.

Nonpeople

There is a small category of people who can break office etiquette without fear. An administrative assistant can walk in and out of the boss's office without knocking. So can maintenance personnel. The reason is that they are *nonpeople*, individuals having no or low organizational status.

In my seminars on professional development for the office workers of a large chemical company, only about 10 percent of the admins say that their boss introduces them by name (rather than as "my assistant") in a meeting. A maintenance person or the plant waterer can enter a meeting room and the conversations will go on without a pause, as if they weren't there.

Waiters and waitresses fall into this same nonperson category. The invisibility of waiters is illustrated by a famous Groucho Marx story. Groucho usually went to Chasen's for dinner after his classic old *You Bet Your Life* tv game show. One evening, some people were celebrating a birthday in an alcove right behind Groucho's booth. When waiters wheeled in a cake, Groucho got up, waved them away, and proceeded to cut the cake himself. He served the cake totally unrecognized by anyone in the alcove, came back to his table, and sat down laughing.

You have heard something like this: "Hello. I'm Ken, and I'll be your waiter for this evening."

"Hello!" you respond, never bothering to introduce yourself. If people introduced themselves to you on the street, would you return the favor? Possibly. You certainly would in a business environment. Then later on, you totally forget the waiter's name. Sometimes you even have trouble remembering who your waiter even was among all the similarly dressed waiters.

The next time you are in a restaurant, introduce yourself back to the waiter or waitress and see what happens. You will have made a "person" out of both yourself and the employee serving you. In the business world, someone you convert from a nonperson to a person will pay back your thoughtfulness tenfold.

Summary

This chapter illustrates the checklist for observing, analyzing, and controlling body location. The checklist shows you how to begin observing NVC by asking the questions:

1. What are the interaction distances? (Territorial Space)
2. What are the height relationships? (Height Might)
3. Who is leading the group? (Tread Spread)
4. Who has the psychological advantage of physical size? (Size Prize)
5. Where is everyone sitting and why? (Seating Dynamics)
6. What respect is shown at the office? (Office Etiquette)

With practice, you will begin to ask yourself these questions automatically, taking only a few moments to accurately size up a new situation. Start finding out how these nonverbal signals apply to your organization. It may seem as if you are looking at your company for the first time, seeing a whole new level of communication. You are, because you are now learning the vocabulary of NVC.

CHAPTER 3

Indicators Scan

SO FAR, YOU HAVE learned to observe and analyze where people put their bodies and why. The second NVC scan involves noting information about people's appearance and environment, including their possessions and ornaments. These points of observation are called *indicators.*

Duration of Indicators

Indicators vary in how long they remain consistent. The first time you meet someone, you will notice a number of pieces of information that you will not need to notice again because they will remain unchanged in later communications sessions. Other indicators will be consistent for only a single communications session. (Remember non-repeatability from Chapter 1.) Still other indicators will not be consistent through even a single communications session.

It is important to separate the indicators you see by their consistency. If you assume a man will always have a mustache and use it to remember his name, you may be in trouble when he shaves it off. A woman student wore a different colored wig and a drastically different outfit the second day of one of my memory classes. Nearly two-thirds of the class had no idea who she was!

Enduring Indicators

Enduring indicators do not change from communications session to communications session. Examples are physical items such as buildings, monuments, and terrain, and personal items such as uniforms. Sometimes, these are more important than the people themselves.

Have you ever been in a store in a suit or dress and had someone come up to you and ask about the location of an item? After you stop and explain that you are also a shopper, the customer walks off glancing over his shoulder with a look that says, "Well, why were you standing there looking like an employee?"

Many locations have gone to the trouble and expense to outfit their employees in order to avoid the confusion. One local hardware chain made a big advertising campaign of having "orange-coated experts" in each of its departments. Their experts were the same old clerks in easily identifiable orange hunter's coats.

A police uniform confers automatic authority on the wearer. At one "enlightened" university, school officials abandoned the campus security uniforms in favor of stylish blazer outfits. Within a few weeks almost the entire force resigned. The officers felt that the blazers made their job harder. They stood out less in a crowd and had less control in a conflict situation. Supervisors felt that the uniforms had given the officers automatic power and focused crowd attention on them, encouraging the officers to act. The school quickly returned to the standard police-style uniform.

Consider the "nonperson" waiter or waitress from the previous chapter. We often forget which waitress is ours because her uniform helps make her a nonperson, just as the maintenance person's getup makes him or her a nonperson to office workers.

I've decided the best way to commit a crime unrecognized is to wear a McDonald's hamburger uniform shirt and pants and sing, "We do it all for you!" Guaranteed, witnesses will see only what I wear and not who I am.

Unusual physical features, such as facial scars, can have the same attention-focusing effect. "What color was the hair, officer?"

"Gee, I don't know. But he did have this horrible scar!"

Physical characteristics may or may not be enduring. The McDonald's disguise is not going to last long after the crime. Hair color, hairstyle, weight, and even facial features may change. So make certain to sort out what you are likely to see again.

Be alert for a change in the norm. Many a spouse has come home and wished that he or she had noticed that new outfit or hairstyle. Don't take anything for granted, in your personal life or in business.

One afternoon, I was calling on a regular customer and waited briefly while he handled a phone call. I noticed a new painting on a wall I had previously seen empty at least 200 times. This made me curious, so I began to scan the room for anything else out of the ordinary.

As I glanced over the large bookcase beside his desk, I noticed a binder with a competitor's name on it, something I had not seen before. It turned out that the customer's entire staff had been to a competitive demonstration versus a product I had recently proposed. I casually asked about the binder's contents and began to compete for a sale I thought was already mine. I may have won the order even if I hadn't seen the binder, but my position would not have been as strong.

Temporary Indicators

Indicators can also be temporary, lasting for only one communications session. Clothing, hairstyle, weather, health, time of day, and location are usually not consistent from session to session. Weather has a tremendous effect on our behavior. Grade school teachers know well that they are in for a long day when there is a steady rain. People who wouldn't even glance in sympathy at a car in a ditch will be out there helping a motorist in a snowstorm.

Some people prefer hot weather and some prefer cold. A friend of mine is a cold-weather person, and can't stand the heat. Put her in a hot room and she will agree to anything to get out.

I would much rather be too warm than too cold. I once taught a four-hour college class in a room adjacent to a boiler. While the rest of the building was down to an energy-conserving 68 degrees (to which everyone was accustomed), our room was in the high 70s. Even though I was on my feet lecturing for four hours, I felt fine after class. The students, however, came out looking like they had spent an afternoon inside a punching bag. So always take into account the weather environment of your session.

Time of day is another important part of people's environment. Some of us are evening people and some are day people. I wake up groggy and don't get going until late morning. I have another period in the day, about 4:00 to 6:00 P.M., that I call my "dead spot," when I am again sluggish. I pick up right after dinner and can go full speed until I drop into bed.

For example, I wrote most of this book after 7:00 P.M. Anyone wanting to sell me something or get my commitment for action would have a tough time during my dead periods. My wife and family recognize this and know to approach me at my best times of day.

Others are day people. These are the bright, eager-to-work, bushy-tailed folks we early groaners hate. Day people usually close up shop early and use the evening hours for relaxation or light work.

I had a sales partner who was like this. As the workload increased, he would come in earlier and earlier, and want me to be there, too. I tried it for a short time, but succeeded only in destroying my entire sleep cycle for several days. I contemplated all kinds of things I could do to him, but I was afraid I would get a "morning" judge after being caught at it.

Certain times of day are bad for *all* people. How do you feel when you sit in a meeting, class, or seminar after lunch? Doesn't it seem like the world is moving in slow motion? Nothing is more miserable than wanting to fall asleep and knowing you can't. I have spent many a class fighting this feeling for two hours every day. The main reason we get sleepy after lunch is that our stomach is robbing our brain of blood.

Be aware of the time factor in your communications sessions. Figure out whether the important people you deal with are night or day people, and in what environment they feel most comfortable. If you don't know, ask them. Maybe you have asked bosses for a raise at the wrong time of the day, or when they are uncomfortable or irritable.

An eager young management trainee I knew could hardly wait for her boss to get in to begin her appraisal. What she didn't know was that his car air conditioner had failed that morning and he showed up for work blazing in more ways than one. Had she postponed the meeting until another day, or at least until he had cooled off, she would have fared much better. Had *he* been sensitive, he would have postponed it. Don't make either mistake by ignoring the time of day and the environment.

Next, start noticing how healthy the other person feels. None of us are effective when we don't feel well. Sales have been lost or raises delayed because the customer or boss had a bad cold.

A more insidious form of "bad health" is having to go to the bathroom. What may come across as impatience may actually be acute pain in trying to avoid the embarrassment of leaving to go to the bathroom.

An executive I know used this as a tactic. He always had lunch brought up during long, intensive planning sessions. Then he would save his ideas until last, when people started getting antsy.

Be aware of the one-time conditions that exist throughout a communications session. Watch and compare what stays constant and what changes. People are influenced by a host of environmental and physical factors, any one of which can have a drastic effect on the messages we send and receive in any given situation. These factors are another reason why communication is not repeatable.

Momentary Indicators

Indicators can also be momentary, lasting only part of the communications session. Examples are distractions, changing locale, visual aids, and even doodles. These momentary items or events can drastically change the course of a session for the better or the worse.

Distractions are the most frequent occurrence. Remember the manager who kept the candy dish in his office? This only increased the candy traffic when the door was open, which led to more door-closed time, and so on. Because of these constant interruptions, his people either avoided talking to him during the day or sought him out before and after regular working hours when they would have a better chance of seeing him with interruption.

The phone is another common distraction. America has a cultural phone-answering compulsion, undoubtedly fostered from the start by Alexander Graham himself. He was no dummy when he designed the device with a ring mechanism. (As comedian George Carlin pointed out, "Isn't it nice that the phone wasn't designed by Alexander Graham Siren?") The baby may be screaming, the sink overflowing, the office on fire, but we'll still answer that incessant ring tone.

All executive training should include a session in *not* answering the phone. Many an important meeting has been wasted by a "short" 20-minute phone call. With one of my managers, who was addicted to phone answering, I would walk out of the room on any phone call lasting more than five minutes.

I always explained leaving with, "Oh, I saw that you were going to be busy and I didn't want to seem like I was listening in. Besides, I had other things to do until you were free."

This attitude has several advantages. First, you aren't reminded of your lowly status by sitting around wasting your time while your boss is handling "more important" work. Second, you are gently urging your boss to stop the practice because you won't "sit still" for it. Finally, you may get a phone call in the meantime that will make the boss wait on you.

There is an effective way to handle a distraction when you are presenting. I was giving a sales presentation-training seminar for a group from a large firm. About a half-hour into my talk, someone came in and made a big commotion settling in. So I shut up. The group finally noticed that I had not been talking about three or four seconds after he sat down.

Not wanting to miss the opportunity, I asked them, "What do you do during a distraction?"

To a person, they answered, "Nothing!"

If your audience, be it one person or many, is distracted, stop and let yourself be distracted, too. When it's over with, their attention will return and your audience will be ready to continue. Like most powerful emotions, curiosity is short-lived. Let it be satisfied before you get back to work.

Beware of changing locale during a session. A young man planned a luncheon date with his boss to discuss his performance and the possibility of a raise. He wisely chose a restaurant where they could talk discreetly, but he made a fatal error in timing. Walking over to the place, his boss innocently asked about the subject of their lunch, and rather than deferring the young man began his prepared talk.

You can imagine the results after dropping off their coats, waiting at the receptionist's table, ordering lunch with frequent visits from the waiter (drink order, drinks, lunch order, lunch, and those eve-

present water and coffee fillers), and chomping on their meals. This critical conversation was never allowed to unfold.

Fortunately, in this instance, the manager wasn't negative. But the young professional accomplished nothing and missed a chance to further himself and his career. The interference of changing location and then eating was too much for the conversation. The ideal time for the conversation would have been *after* lunch. They both would have been relaxed and the manager softened up.

As a rule, don't change locations. If you have to move, always move to a *better* location for communication. A good example is eating dinner then going to a different room for a presentation, or getting people out of their personal territory and into a neutral area or into your territory. The best approach is to control the timing of your communications so that the location can become a temporary environment rather than a momentary one.

Any group of visuals, whether formal aids or extemporaneous doodles, are momentary indicators. There is a wealth of NVC material in visuals. A useful trick in meetings is to be the last one to leave so that you can look at the doodles on all the remaining pads. If it is your meeting, make sure there are pads to use and that you leave last. If you are merely an attendee and can't leave last, make sure to take all your papers with you so you don't provide any unplanned insight into your reactions to the content.

One time, employees of a radio station in Florida were caught by police going through a rival station's trash. Station personnel had managed to piece together an entire promotional campaign from meeting notes taken during planning sessions. Because of the bad publicity generated by the arrest, the station was forced to return the material, but it still gained a marketing coup. Don't let one of *your* rivals do the same.

A visual aid is a special, controlled type of distraction. It takes attention away from you, so you must return the favor for it to be effective. I once saw visuals so concise that anyone would have looked knowledgeable using them. The audience realized it and gave due credit to the presenter who developed them. I have also seen visuals that looked as if they had been drawn by a elementary schooler. The audience was equally unimpressed with the speaker using them.

Remember that visuals should be used only when words and body alone are not as effective. They are a distraction with a purpose. Make sure you are presenting your visuals instead of vice versa.

Identifying indicators is really an exercise in increasing your skills of observation. Once you are familiar with the important indicators of the people you deal with, you can sort the indicators by their consistency. Some will be constant throughout your acquaintance with the person. Some will last only during a session. And a few will vary from moment to moment.

Types of Indicators
There are three types of indicators you can use as a checklist:
Personal
Shared
Public

As the names imply, these indicators vary with respect to how large a group they provide information about. Personal indicators apply to individuals. Shared indicators apply to a group such as a company or a club. And public indicators apply to a large group, usually related geographically.

Personal Indicators
If there is one common trait exhibited by humanity, it is the overwhelming drive to decorate its nest. I have not been in a single office that was not in some way customized by its occupant. Even in sparsely decorated offices, some form of humanizing has taken place.

Possessions and Decor
My sales office was a good example of the way people personalize their surroundings. All the desks were out in the middle of big, open rooms, set side by side with only two-drawer file cabinets separating them. Each desk was equipped with a phone. (This unappealing environment may have been intentional—to keep the salespeople out of the office—but I suspect that it was also inexpensive.) Despite the antiseptic atmosphere, each desk was in some way personalized. Managers had small nameplates posted on the front of their desks, but the names weren't really needed. The belongings and parapher-

nalia on each desk were enough to immediately identify whose desk it was.

There were bookends with an abundance of work-related books. There were trophies and awards from contests and classes. And there were those miscellaneous little items that are the most revealing.

My desk had a chunk of artificial turf with a little Miami Dolphins helmet on it to ward off the old St. Louis Cardinal football fans. I also had a *Ziggy* cartoon saying, "Today is a whole new day to screw up in," in honor of my usual status with management. Another cartoon, a reminder of my first commission check, featured Seminole Sam of *Pogo* bragging that he at one time had amassed a fortune of $24.60 in due bills.

Other desks had such things as a soldered-nail basketball player, a plastic Charlie the Tuna radio, plants, United Van Lines toy trucks, mistake erasers, family picture cubes, a toy mailbox, and a boat on a bendable wire.

Many items were even useful. I had an artificial turf telephone pad so my desk phone would sound different from the 20 or so adjacent phones. There was a myriad of phone number holders, appointment books, and phone note holders. Each desk was truly a reflection of its owner.

Even the trash around the desk was indicative of the person who used it. Look around your office and you will probably come up with a list of items as wacky as the one above. Though the salespeople in my office spent only a small portion of their time at their desks, a great deal of personalizing was still in evidence.

There was even more individualization in the managerial offices. In addition to desk paraphernalia, almost every wall and piece of furniture had some personal touch. Paintings and pictures were in abundance. Managers were sure to include anything of status in their gallery of framed pictures. Boat pictures are good, if the boat is big. A picture of the office occupant standing beside his or her airplane is even better.

The most impressive personal picture of this type belonged to the chief of pilots of a regional airline company. The picture showed him standing on the con of a nuclear sub—a duty he had pulled during his reserve summer tour. How many people do you know who have been aboard a nuclear sub *on duty*?

Paintings are also a good source of information about the occupant's tastes. At the very least, they are conversation pieces. Be careful, though, in making comments about a painting or work of art. You can offend even if you intend to compliment.

I once stuck my foot in my mouth with incredible grace and speed by trying to be nice. I complimented an executive on a painting he had displayed, only to find out that he had just moved into the office and hated the painting, but hadn't had time to do anything about it. Paintings often grow old or stale to the person living in the office. The best thing to do if you want to talk about a painting is to ask a question about it rather than offering a blind comment.

Degrees, certificates, and awards are other effective wall decorations. They will tell you what the occupant's activities are and what he or she is proud of. They usually come in the standard 8-1/2" x 11" size and are displayed in clusters.

If you wish to display some of these in your office, make certain they create a positive effect. For example, when I left my sales position, I had two plaques and certificates of achievement for making my company's 100 percent quota club. When I left my island desk to set up my own office, I decided to decorate my work area with some of these items. When I put my four items on the wall, they looked naked, almost obscene. I had seen managers with a string of them running from floor to ceiling in their offices. My little display was totally underwhelming.

Decorations can be overdone too. I visited a business consultant who had approximately 25 framed documents on his office wall. When I noncommittally mentioned them, he apologized for the number, telling me that there were four more being framed!

This display might have been awe-inspiring, except that he had obviously mounted every document he had ever received. There were fraternal awards of the kind that are passed out like pancakes (an Optimist Club executive calls them "M&Ms for the troops"). There were also letters of appreciation, certificates of membership, and one or two outstanding meeting awards. The net effect was to appear ostentatious and ridiculous.

As a rule of thumb, the properly impressive number of framed business items is five to eight. The typical mixture might include two Degrees from Somewhere, a couple of Certified Professional Somethings, and a Member of the Year Award from the Affiliated Associates Association. Make sure they are in the same style of frame so that their number, rather than content, is what strikes the visitor.

Unique or bizarre decorations are also status grabbers. Imagine the company president asking you about the African witchdoctor's mask hanging on your wall. How can he top you when you answer, "Oh, I picked that little thing up on my last trip to the continent"? You know all he's had time for is the stockholders' meeting in Attumswa, Iowa.

Items that are totally unfathomable have the same effect. Prominently display some unimaginable object at the front of your desk. Natural curiosity will force your visitors to ask what it is, in which case you are one up on them. If they don't ask about it, idly play with it as you talk. You will at least distract them, giving yourself a further advantage.

A hot item with the computer folks was a printer counterweight, a heavy cylindrical piece of metal that slid in and out of a plastic sleeve. It had no reasonable purpose, but its moving parts gave it a high fondle value.

Puzzles are also good for maintaining control over your callers. I had one customer who kept a small block puzzle on his desk for this very purpose. I studiously ignored it, being careful not to even look at it lest that allow my customer to bring it up.

One day he caught me when we started talking about a mutual hobby, puzzles. He suddenly told me, "Well, if you like puzzles, why don't you try this one?" and shoved the block at me. Then he held up his arm and started looking at his watch, saying, "I just want to see how long it takes you; don't mind me."

As all of us who have stood before a group in silence know, a minute can be interminable. I managed to get the block assembled after two and a half minutes, which rated, "That's not too bad, Ken." Before I was buried in any more condescending remarks, I cut the meeting short and beat a hasty retreat.

Before the next call on this customer, I memorized a set of ten pencil-and-paper logic puzzles. I resolved that if stumped again, I would at least be able to *trade* puzzles. So beware of any desk puzzles you see. They can be used to inflict major psychological damage.

Appearance

We all place a tremendous amount of importance on physical appearance. Not only does it provide basic demographic data on age, gender, height, weight, and physical beauty, it also provides a wealth of data on personality. Appearance is so important to use that we have a special term for our initial analysis of it—the first impression.

First Impressions

A first impression is the "love at first sight" of the business world. We know the importance of making a good first impression, since we "never have a second chance to make a good first impression." Yet so few of us know what first impression we give.

I use a first-impression fact-finding procedure in my communications classes. As each person introduces himself or herself at the beginning of the class, the students write on a note card five traits they think best describe this person. When the introductions are completed, the cards are distributed to the attendees. They then have a database of first-impression traits from their peers, given anonymously.

Frequently, the cards are quite similar in content and provide a good composite of the first impression the student creates. Grouping similar adjectives, such as intelligent/smart/quick or ambitious/aggressive/go-getter, gives an even better composite picture. A refinement in this first-impression procedure is to have class members write down what caused them to list a certain trait for a student. This gives the student valuable feedback.

Clothing has an enormous effect on the first impression you project. John T. Molloy has analyzed the effect of various types of men's and women's clothing in his books on "wardrobe engineering." Almost all his research methods were based on first impressions. He showed different clothing styles to individuals and then asked them to draw conclusions about the people wearing the clothes. Molloy's *Dress for Success* and *The Woman's Dress for Success Book* offer valuable information on clothing styles in business.

It is well worth your time to find out the first impression you send out. If you don't have an opportunity to use the classroom method of introduction, ask one of your close friends to give you a candid assessment. Or have a friend find out for you by informally questioning your associates. Try to tie the impressions back to specific characteristics or traits, and don't be defensive!

Body Types

You can also benefit by appraising your physical characteristics for data on your appearance and how that affects how people perceive you. Like it or not, people tend to culturally stereotype others based on body type. And there are physical issues that can affect a person's NVC message.

There are three different body types: ectomorph, endomorph, and mesomorph.

Ectomorphs are below average in weight for their height, and have a narrow frame. They have fast metabolisms and can eat whatever they want. They may have difficulty gaining weight and building muscle.

Ectomorphs can appear to be tense and nervous. Their gestures are more accentuated because of their slender frame, and they can seem to be moving faster and less smoothly. Classic comedian Don Knotts exaggerated this in his "nervous" character routine. It was a terrible shock to see him on an evening talk show speaking normally.

There are several ways to deal with a slender image. Don't accentuate your thinness with clothing. Ignore form-fitting clothing. Stay away from vertically striped fabrics. Coats should be cut fuller (but not baggy). Vests can add bulk. Ties should be as wide as fashionable, without making you look like Corky the Clown. Avoid sleeveless tops since they focus attention on the arms.

Another tip is to slow down. Gesture less rapidly, walk slower, and in general give the image of care and forethought. Make your gestures more muted. If you have a nervous habit such as nail biting, finger twisting, or cuticle picking, concentrate on eliminating it. With this body style, habits like these will be magnified and reinforce the nervous stereotype.

The second body type is the endomorph. This person is often above average in weight, and has a larger frame. They have slower metabolisms, and cannot seem to lose weight. And they often tire easily.

Stereotypically, endomorphs are considered to be good-natured and jolly, with an untiring sense of humor. (Think Santa Claus.) They are shorter and stockier, and can easily gain both muscle and fat.

Endomorphs often have a more difficult time looking neat. Today's styles are not necessarily made for larger people to wear comfortably. Shirts or blouses pull out at the waist, pants or slacks ride up as people sit down. And all the constrictions around the neck, arms, and legs accentuate any loose skin. It takes constant attention to look sharp.

For example, an endomorph salesman made a habit of stopping by the men's room in any office building where he was going to make a call. He would straighten himself out after the car ride and then proceed. He felt that taking this time to neaten up his appearance was important to his image. He never walked into an office with his hair blown, tie crooked, collar up, or shoes muddy. You shouldn't either.

The third body type is the in-between person—the mesomorph. These are the people with athletic builds, the kind that adorn our daytime serials and fill up Muscle Beach.

When I was in college, there was a standing joke about guys who went out for track, which was my sport. When all the athletes came in to take showers in the afternoon after their workouts, you could tell each one's sport by his behavior.

The football players would come in, bend the showerhead pipe to the proper angle, soap themselves up, and begin throwing soap at everybody. The basketballers would come in and loop their towels over the water pipes near the ceiling. The wrestlers would come in looking like little Mr. Americas, wishing they could drink the water instead of wash in it. The baseballers would amble in, every pore of their bodies oozing coordination. The skinny, scrawny guys who didn't look like any sort of athlete? They were the trackmen.

The problem for trackmen was that everyone else in the shower, even most of the basketball players, were those irritating mesomorphs. They were the ones who best filled out their letter jackets, and had muscles where trackmen didn't even have places.

Don't underestimate the advantage that a mesomorph possesses in the world of NVC. In the 1976 presidential campaign, former President Ford proudly stated that he could still hike a football and fire off the line just as he did years ago at Michigan. And the public believed him. Unlike many Presidents, Ford skied, swam, and played golf. He left office as fit as or more fit than when he went in.

Mesomorphs come off as more self-reliant, more mature. Many top executives of major companies are mesomorphs—perhaps as high as

80 to 90 percent in some organizations. Do they fit this mold in your company? Do you?

If you do, don't destroy it. Stay in shape—not only for your image, but for your personal health. There is a definite relationship between a sound body and business success. With all the fitness options out there today, you should be able to find something that interests you. Find it and develop it into a habit!

With all this said, it is common that people are a mix of two body types... mesomorph with ectomorph or endomorph. Ectomorphs can build lean muscle mass. And endomorphs can optimize their diet and get ripped, too.

Whatever your body style, be aware of what your physical appearance transmits. Begin to think of body style as a changeable trait, not a permanent feature. If you don't like your current equipment, now is the time to start modifying it. If you don't want to put out the effort to change yourself, at least analyze what you are and minimize any negative effects through clothing and grooming. Give your body real "style" and you will have another NVC plus.

Shared Indicators

Shared indicators include large, immovable, or difficult-to-move objects such as offices, desks, statues, and bookcases.

Michael Korda, in his book *Power,* makes a detailed study of the relationships of office location and status. He points out that corner offices reflect the most power and status within an organization.

The architect for the original Community Federal Savings and Loan building in St. Louis incorporated this idea into the design. To make it a more attractive lease property in the highly competitive St. Louis office-space market, the architect provided more corner offices than the conventional square or rectangular structure. (See Figure 3–1.)

Office size and furnishings are also indicative of status. I have never seen a subordinate's office better furnished than a manager's office if the two are physically close to each other. Even if the subordinate has a larger office, the manager's office is usually better located.

Many organizations have a special "executive's row" with limited access through a screening secretary. Most managers would rather take a cut in salary than pass up a chance to join the row.

One large utility went so far as to locate its top executives in a different building, a plush office in the downtown business area a mile or so from the main location. The corporate officers and the two executive vice-presidents were the only occupants of the facility and had almost half a floor of space. This was the ultimate in status. Even subordinates at the vice-presidential level had to get in their car, fight traffic, park, and make their way to the executive offices for any meeting. The top executives *never* went to the main office building.

In addition, the main headquarters building was constructed with metal walls and partitions. The nicest office in the building still looked like the inside of a refrigerator, while the executive suites had more wood in them than a lumber dealer. The working environment reinforced the higher status of the office occupants.

Desks are another status indicator. At the lower levels, size is the important feature. The bigger your desk, the greater your status. Ideally, I suppose, you should have a desk that looks like a roller rink.

At the higher levels, size is often a minor factor, with simplicity taking precedence. As noted earlier, some chief executives are doing

Figure 3–1. Corner-office building.

(Courtesy Community Federal Savings and Loan Association, St. Louis, Missouri)

away with the business desk and installing ornate tables of the same size. This is similar to the executive who doesn't wear a timepiece, which says in effect, "I don't have to worry about what time it is. My assistants will keep me informed, or everyone else will have to conform to my schedule regardless of the time."

A drawerless table says much the same thing. "I don't have to store materials for retrieval, nor do I do the type of work that requires me to dig into papers all over my desk." This executive will keep a simple office with a clean desk at all times.

Books are another shared indicator that provides a great deal of information about the owner. I recently met with the chairman of a management program in a local university. As I walked in, I noticed massive bookshelves lining one wall. We were interrupted briefly by the phone after I sat down, so I spent the time looking at the titles on the shelf. I was surprised that the chairman of a management program would have so many finance-oriented books.

When our conversation resumed, I opened with, "How did you manage to switch from a finance professorship to chair a management department?"

He began to answer and suddenly stopped, asking, "How did you know that?"

I explained about the evidence on the shelves, and he gave me one of Dr. Watson's frequent comments to Sherlock Holmes, "Oh, that's obvious. Why didn't I think of it?"

Bookshelf ogling is easy and is an excellent way to learn the tastes and interests of the owner of the books. It is also a good way to build rapport with a new acquaintance during those first awkward minutes. One small warning, though.

Don't be tempted to load up *your* shelves with impressive titles you have never read. If you are asked about one of the books you've never opened, you expose yourself as a fake. So choose books you have read or at least know about, selecting the books to represent the image you wish to project.

If you are a young college grad don't throw your old college textbooks up there. You're trying to project maturity and good judgment. Stick to business-oriented books from well-known authors.

If you want to project intelligence, go heavy on psychology and esoterica with big-worded titles that no one has ever heard of. Quoting from these books will also help maintain your image.

One manager I encountered decided to go with the "intelligence" image. He loaded his office with classical paintings, "heavy" books, strange desk puzzles, and obscure sayings. He was indeed intelligent and emphasized the point well. Eventually he was promoted to a job in a development division where intelligence and creativity were requirements for success. He used his personal and shared indicators to help create the image necessary for his promotion.

Public Indicators

Public indicators are the things around us that are not only shared, but that are also open to the general public. Examples are houses, museums, monuments, shopping centers, highways, buildings, stadiums, and parks. These are indicative of our culture and of our living habits. Certain public artifacts are also good measures of social status, and can communicate a great deal about an individual.

For example, where we live is a factor. A successful executive had very strong ideas about buying a house. He felt he should buy one that he would be better able to afford in three years. The house should be the lowest-priced house in a high-priced neighborhood and big enough so that he would not have to move out unless he was transferred (in which case the company would pay). The house he bought has doubled in value and is worth approximately 75 percent as much as the average house in his area. More important, he lives in *the* neighborhood in his city, one whose average house costs far more than what people at his job level normally pay.

It turned out that the small corporation he works for hired a new president from the outside, over the current line of executives. The new president, unfamiliar with the area and buying within his salary, bought a suitable house in the city. He later found out that our executive had a better house and was located in a more exclusive area. Now the executive loves to entertain his boss and associates in his home whenever possible.

I once interviewed for a position at a manufacturing plant nestled in a mountain valley 70 miles from the nearest city with a population over 50,000. The entire social life of the area centered around the plant activities and a country club with a nine-hole golf course. Membership in the club was restricted to executives and managers from the plant. I was supposed to be totally impressed when I was offered a membership if I went to work at the plant, since this was the highest status I could hope to attain in the area.

Just as certain areas of a city have more status than others, so some cities are considered more prestigious than others. Anyone born and living outside of New York has felt the patronizing attitude of those inhabitants of the nation's largest city. New York becomes a source of "war stories" for outsiders. Mastering its customs is a rite of passage for the newcomer.

A friend of mine who moved there from a Midwestern city was driving like a madman within a year. He would trample beggars without breaking stride and had a wealth of "New York stories" to pass on to us country bumpkins. As proof of the status he'd gained, he would be asked on his trips back to the Midwest, "What's it like up there?"

A Contrarian Thought

At this point, after reading this chapter, you may have had a very common reaction. "What a bunch of BS. How sad is it that people are insecure enough that they have to impress other people with what they wear, what they put around them, or where they live? What happened to the idea of showing up for work in business casual, and just being great at what you do? Who cares how things look?"

And you are perfectly right to feel that way. In a rational, performance-oriented world, the quality of a person's work should be all that matters. But for many people, that is not the case.

They are not only looking at your work. They are looking at the total visual package in their evaluation. That includes not only your performance, but also you and the environment you create around you. And if you are being honest with yourself, you are making similar judgments when you size people up. All these indicators are providing information on people's personality and status.

Summary

Chapter 2 presented the first NVC checklist for observing and controlling where people put their bodies and why. This chapter introduced the checklist for interpreting indicators such as people's appearance and what they put around them. In analyzing yourself and others for these nonverbal indicators, try to answer the following questions:

1. What are people's possessions and appearance characteristics? (Personal Indicators)
2. What items do people have in common? (Shared Indicators)
3. What categories or groups do people fit into? (Public Indicators)

The key to success with all indicators is observation. Take every opportunity to observe the objects around the people you communicate with. Look at the desk, the furniture, the office. Find out where a person lives and why. The more you understand about how a person decorates his or her nest and why it is located where it is, the better you will understand the person.

CHAPTER 4

Body Movements Scan

THE STUDY OF BODY motions, called "kinesics" (from the Greek word for "movement"), is a relatively new science. Begun in the early 1950s by a researcher named Birdwhistell, and popularized by Julius Fast in his book *Body Language*, kinesics has historically had little application to the workplace. Until now, its principles have not been organized into an easy-to-apply method. Such a method is now available with the five-point body scan which consists of:

1. Center
2. Head
3. Posture
4. Hands
5. Legs

This body scan will help you to "hear better with your glasses on." It lets you observe others in an organized head-to-toe fashion.

Although interpretations will be given for various NVC signals, it is important to keep in mind that *each item in the scan must be checked before any conclusions can be drawn*. As the example from Chapter 1 showed with the customer who covered his mouth, movements are not traits. This leads to the major rule: **No one sign in and of itself is indicative of anything.**

Reliable signals come in *clusters*. There is no one nonverbal sign that is subliminally giving away some giant secret. Signs will tend to be multiple, and they will agree with each other. It is a matter of context. When someone has a particular attitude, it will come out in a number of ways. The more of them you see, the stronger the read.

But this is not a particularly severe limitation. Most situations include enough movement indicators to allow you to draw at least broad conclusions—unless people are purposely trying to cover up their feelings. Even that is a nonverbal signal, usually followed by the question, "Is there something wrong?"

So here is the sequence you can use in reading someone's body position and movements.

1. Center

Imagine a rod going through the middle of your chest to the middle of your shoulder blades. Then imagine another rod from armpit to armpit. Where these imaginary rods connect in your chest is your "center," as shown in Figure 4–1.

The center is perhaps the most reliable and important body indicator. It is the only sign that can ever be successfully taken out of context, and is a key indicator of how we feel about ourselves, and about the others around us.

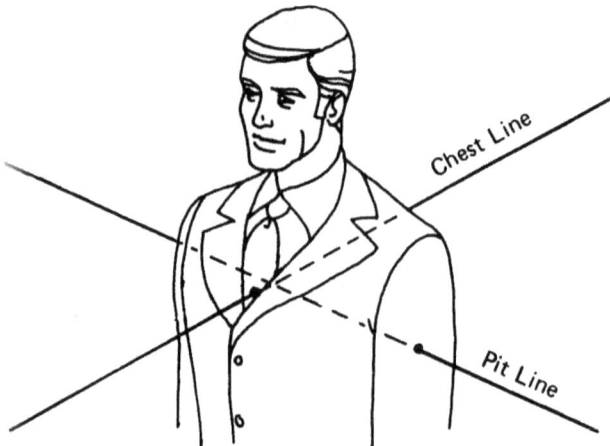

Figure 4–1. The center.

The center can be open or closed, and aggressive or submissive.

We achieve an open center by standing erect and facing the person we are communicating with.

We close our center by buttoning our coat or blazer, slumping, crossing our arms in umpire fashion, sitting with a chair back facing forward, or turning away from the person to talk over our shoulder.

Our center becomes aggressive with our chest out, shoulders back, and chin out, much like a Marine sergeant hazing his "boots."

Our center becomes submissive when it is "buried" with bent posture, bowed shoulders, and a downcast gaze.

Occasionally, I'll begin a lecture by walking in front of the group slumped over, picking at my cuticles, and offering in a halting voice, "W-w-well, I'm the communicator. I'm here to teach you how to be effective like I am." You can hear a groan go through the audience as they glance around to spot the doors best suited for an inconspicuous exit.

Or I may walk in with body erect, coat buttoned, and arms stiffly held at the sides, stiffly and announcing in a monotone, "Hello, I'm Ken Cooper. I am your friend because—I care. You can tell me your problems in complete confidence and know I will help." With this introduction, I can see lips and tongues being bitten all over the room with the thought, "Oh, no, what have I gotten myself into?"

Other times I stride out with coat open, chest thrust out, arms clasped behind my back, and aggressively state, "I'm Ken Cooper. You're going to like this class because you need this class. We will have one ten-minute break in the morning and one in the afternoon, and that is all because we have a lot to do. Are there any questions?" There never are, of course, because they are too busy trying to see if I am armed.

After each of these shocks, I revert to my normal self and begin talking about what my varied approach made them think about me and the coming talk. Yes, my movements involved more than manipulating my center. But most students later agree that the center is a key indicator.

In general, an open center indicates a friendly, positive attitude toward a person. Conversely, a closed center is negative. Shake hands with someone face to face, and then shake hands with your shoulders pointing at the person looking over your right shoulder. See how less friendly the second position is? Stand in front of a mirror and note how much more informal and open you look with your jacket or blazer unbuttoned.

Notice how people orient their centers when sitting at meetings. When two rival executives are placed in adjacent chairs, they will almost always sit with their shoulders angled away from each other, possibly with legs crossed so that their up foot points away from the unfriendly neighbor. They are closing off to each other.

A child psychologist told me he always has both parents come with their child to the first meeting. He observes the parents in the lobby before the appointment. If the parents are sitting with their centers open, possibly with the husband's arm around his wife or at least turned toward each other, the psychologist spends most of the first meeting talking with the child. If the parents are closed to each other as they sit or do not sit next to each other, or if one of them sits with the child while the other sits across from the two, the psychologist spends his initial time probing to see what problems there are between the parents that could be affecting the child.

The orientation of the center is also an indicator of territorial space. When someone is too close, people tend to close their center off to that person, creating a bit of a barrier.

Conversely, we can be threatened by an open center when standing next to a stranger. As Figure 4–2 shows, opening our center intensifies our need for territorial space.

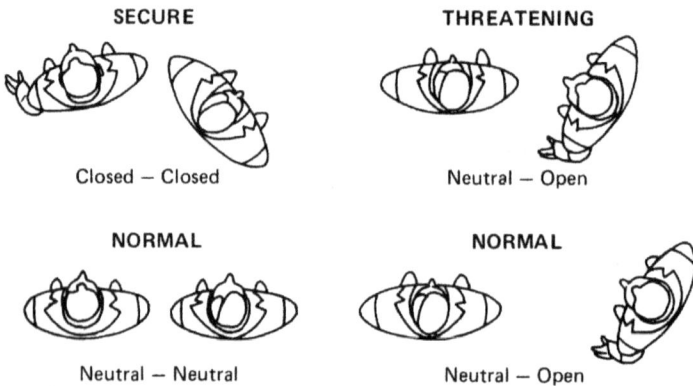

SECURE

THREATENING

Closed — Closed

Neutral — Open

NORMAL

NORMAL

Neutral — Neutral

Neutral — Open

Figure 4–2. Public centers.

A short comment about the crossed-arms method of closing off the center is needed here. Most books report that this is always a negative sign.

I believe that crossed arms is a totally overrated sign. It is just a comfortable thing to do with your arms. Maybe you are cold. Maybe you are trying to surreptitiously rearrange an undergarment. Maybe your underarms itch. Maybe it's just learned behavior. But it is such a common habitual gesture that you cannot consider it a reliable signal on its own. You need further correlated reads for it to be meaningful.

I saw an incident that reinforced this when I was downtown shopping during the holiday season. A woman was standing at a bus stop with her three-year-old daughter. The mother was waiting impatiently, shifting from one foot to the other, arms crossed, with an exasperated expression on her face.

As I walked down the sidewalk, I saw the little girl, who was standing in the rumpled manner of little girls everywhere, look up and study her mother. Glancing quickly back and forth from her own body to her mother's, she slowly crossed her arms, shifted her weight, and when she was certain she "had it right," stood triumphantly in the exact same pose as her mother, in other words, learned behavior.

So more than most other NVC signs, crossed arms, by themselves, means *nothing*.

Center orientations can also indicate people's relationships within groups. In Figure 2-1, for example, the "choir effect" and "outsider" configurations were primarily indicated by people's centers in addition to their territorial space. The three subordinates encircling the leader all had their centers oriented to the boss. The person "out" of the informal circle was closed off by the people on either side.

As you become more aware of centers, you will be able to read people's open and closed attitudes toward others, and their aggressive and submissive attitudes about themselves.

2. Head
It is rod time again. Imagine a rod going through that open alley your friends claim connects your ears. Then imagine another rod going straight back into your head through the tip of your nose.

If you can picture these rods providing axes of rotation for the head, you can see how you can nod up and down around the first axis, and tilt left and right about the second axis. As Figure 4–3 shows, the ear rod is your Self axis, and the nose rod is your Others axis.

By rotating about these lines, the head can assume four basic positions.

If the head is rotated upward around the Self line, you are showing *superiority* ("looking down your nose" at someone). Author and TV personality William F. Buckley frequently appeared to hold his head in this position.

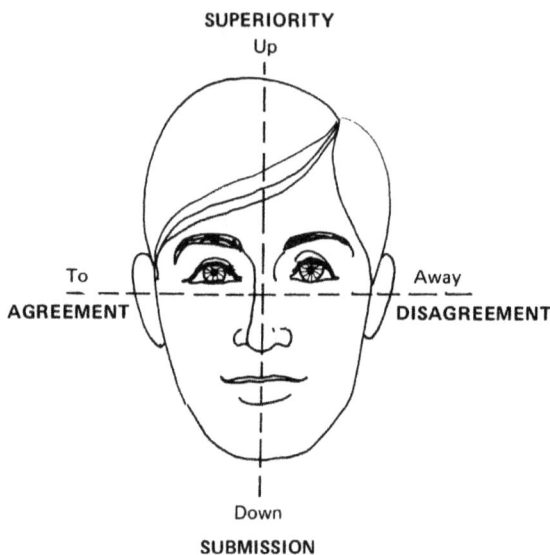

Figure 4–3. Head positions.

If your head rotates downward, you are showing *submission* ("hanging your head").

If your head is tilted around the others line toward someone, you are indicating *agreement*.

If it is tilted away, you are indicating *disagreement*.

Tilting the head with the center open can indicate other things besides agreement. Often it is a sign of *attention*. (Remember King Kong holding Fay Wray with his head tilted, thinking "Hmmm"?)

Many people unconsciously tilt their head when they are trying to listen more closely (listening with an "ear cocked"). The tilt can also be a sign of *evaluation* or *deep thought*.

As we are thinking, we tilt our head and gaze into space with unfocused eyes while the brain churns. Or at least that's what we want people to think. I sometimes utilize this "deep thought" pose after being asked a difficult question in a class. I may know the answer immediately, but my response will be more credible if I appear to be work for it. Besides, it is a compliment to the questioner to honor his or her query with such effort.

Watch how you position your head. Is your normal position neutral? Some of us assume a dominant or submissive position out of habit. As we saw in the section on height might, unconscious habits can influence the way people view us. People resent those who have their "nose in the air." So "keep a level head about you" and watch when others don't.

3. Facial Expressions

The syndicated column "Fables of the Famous" tells the story about the French novelist Balzac's first visit to Vienna. He was not familiar with either the language or the money, and was afraid he was being overcharged whenever he traveled by taxi. To make certain that he would not be "taken" on his trips, he developed a simple payment procedure based on the driver's face.

Upon arriving, he would hand the driver a single coin. If the driver's hand remained out expectantly, he would add another coin. He kept adding one at a time until the driver smiled. Then Balzac would take back the last coin and depart, confident that he had paid the proper fare and no more! He was the novelist equivalent of Clever Hans the horse.

Our face is the most expressive part of our body—something Balzac's taxi drivers clearly didn't appreciate. In fact, Birdwhistell estimated that, with all the possible elements in a face, we can make and recognize nearly 250,000 distinct facial expressions. Most researchers recognize the following as the most common:

Interest/excitement	Shame/humiliation
Enjoyment/joy	Contempt/disgust
Surprise/startlement	Anger/rage
Distress/anguish	Fear/terror

Retail clerks have their die-cast smiles and sales personnel have their hearty personalities, no matter how bad the day has been. But an old saying warns, "Beware of someone who laughs without a shaking belly." We can mask with muscular control (poker face) or with a prop (toupee, wig, or colored contact lenses). We can choose to accentuate certain characteristics that overshadow others, like Jimmy Durante always posing in profile. (No one seems to have ever noticed the color of Jimmy Durante's eyes.)

When we do show emotions, we often display them in *partials*, reacting with only a portion of the face. I had a regional manager who was the most unconvincing liar I have ever met. He frightened everybody in the office because whenever he praised our sales, he smiled only with his mouth. When he told us how much better we were going to do next year (or else), he showed it with his entire face.

Sometimes we let our emotions out in uncontrollable "flashes." I was sitting at my desk one afternoon when someone from outside the sales office came in to use the phone. I glanced up and, not recognizing the woman, went back to my work. She caught my glance and said, "Well, hi, Ken. I haven't seen you for quite a while."

I looked up again, still not recognizing her, until the sound of her voice told me who she was—a customer I had not seen for nearly 18 months. My confusion arose because when I had seen her last, she had carried about 380 pounds on a 5'2" frame. The woman I was looking at must have weighed 200 pounds less.

Being the cool, suave, controlled NVC expert that I am, my jaw dropped open and I managed an unintelligible, "Huh? Wha? Joan?" It took long seconds for the shock to pass and my brain to associate the New Joan with the old version in memory.

I later apologized for acting so stupid, but she was very gracious about it. She told me, "Don't worry about it, Ken. It's the nicest compliment you could have paid me. Besides, I like to see salesmen speechless occasionally." This was a pleasant, but rather unnerving facial flash.

Facial Indicators

One of the reasons expression is so easy to read and difficult to control is that it is made up of eight different factors: forehead, brows, lids, eyes, nose, lips, chin, and skin.

Forehead

The forehead is a great indicator of physical and emotional states. A furrowed brow, read along with other facial features, can indicate puzzlement, deep thought, tension, worry, fear, or concern. A sweating forehead may indicate effort or nervousness.

A naturally wide forehead or one due to a receding hairline often adds strength of character to the face. A small forehead or one hidden by hair gives a younger, more casual appearance.

Eyebrows

Eyebrows can be very expressive. They can be furrowed, heavy, light, penciled, soft, or a myriad of other adjectives spelled out in romantic novels. The brows tend to soften or harden a face.

John F. Kennedy, for example, had what scientists call "medially downturned eyebrows," which gave his face a concerned look even at rest. Imagine JFK with Everett Dirksen's bushy eyebrows of down-to-earth experience.

Thin, penciled eyebrows give a more mature, hardened look. Arched brows are more dramatic. Light eyebrows on either a man or a woman give the face a softer quality, lacking presence. The vertical line between the brows help form a concerned, worried look.

Eyebrow movement can indicate a variety of emotional states. Our brows may move up suddenly with surprise, fear, or recognition, or they may move down forcefully to indicate concern, worry, or anger. Richard Nixon's overhanging brows give him that brooding, sinister look that political cartoonists loved.

Eyelids

Eyelids are primarily indicators of alertness or involvement. People who have that sleepy or hooded look are thought to be cool, slow-moving, in control, and detached. An overlong gaze with lids lowered can show sexual interest. Bright-eyed, or wide-eyed people often have a look of alertness, innocence, or wonder.

Examples of these two extremes are Charles Bronson and Eddie Cantor. And Asians have an epicanthic skin fold around the eye, which gives it a more closed look.

The wink is a useful NVC device. It can mean "Okay" or "Hi, cute person," or it can be a warming personal gesture. Many of today's "yuk and chuckle" newscasters make this their main tool for exhibiting warmth and charisma. A wink can leer if it is broad enough, or it can point out that the previous statement was sarcastic. A very long wink will almost guarantee a laugh from any crowd because it is a burlesque of the "smooth mover."

Eyes

Important as the eyelids, brows, and forehead are, they all pale in significance compared with the eyes. The eyes indeed have it. Often called "the windows of the soul," they indicate the object of our attention. You know how mad you get when someone wears dark glasses indoors? You are uncomfortable because the other person has the distinct advantage of being able to look anywhere unobserved. Dark glasses allow people to break the unwritten rules of eye contact.

By school age, most children have learned the basic rules of public eye contact. Throughout their early years, they have been told, "It's not polite to stare," "Don't look at that man while he's eating," or "Keep your eyes to yourself."

In the area of "public looking time," it's called *civil inattention*. This is the practice of letting your gaze rest momentarily on strangers before moving on after a decent period of time. That time can vary from group to group and situation to situation, but it is usually about one second long. As we walk along the sidewalk, our gaze will flicker randomly from face to face in civil inattention timespans, our expression never changing. At a party, civil inattention time is extended slightly as people size each other up.

If we look too long at a stranger, we are guilty of *immoral looking time*. We can show interest or challenge someone by maintaining too much eye contact. If you walk along the same street resting your gaze for immoral looking times, you can cause people to avert their eyes. Or you may find others challenging your gaze by staring back belligerently as if to say (as in the battery commercial), "You want to start something?"

Sexual interest can also be shown by lingering eye contact. In fact, one of the six levels of sexual harassment is Aesthetic Appreciation, where an offender maintains an uncomfortably long gaze on the target.

People also practice the *shift-away* on certain classes of people. One of my students, a woman paralyzed from the waist down and confined to a wheelchair, told me about the way people handle eye contact with her. The minute she notices people looking at her, they quickly avert their eyes so "she won't think they are staring."

She said this is worse than being stared at. Can you imagine going through life with people constantly looking away from you as you meet their eyes, and then trying to sneak a peek when they think you aren't looking? You end up never having eye contact with anyone. The most human thing to do is to practice civil inattention here too, letting your eyes rest for the normal brief interval before moving on.

The most uncomfortable version of public eye contact is the *nonperson stare*. The nonperson stare does not grant the other person enough status to deserve civil inattention. It "looks right through you," as if you weren't there. Examples are the hate stare of prejudice or the blank stare waiters or waitresses as diners talk at their table.

Then there is "private looking time" which is vastly different from public looking time, because eye contact is expected to go up when we talk to people we know. The degree of eye contact in a conversation can often vary from 25 percent to 100 percent, depending on who is talking. Eye contact is reduced when we are doing the talking, and is dramatically increased when we are listening—going from a normal 40 percent to 60 percent for talking to an average of 80 percent for listening. Too much eye contact can again become dominating.

A manager I once knew maintained almost total eye contact whether he was speaking or listening. It was as if he came out of a basket to the tune of an Indian flute. If his eyes had spiraled, he could have starred as Kaa the Snake in Disney's *Jungle Book*. Everyone was uncomfortable in this manager's presence, and felt intimidated in staring back at him or in trying to furtively look away. In addition, this manager was very tall and had a nonexistent intimate territorial space. Ten minutes with this man standing closely over you and staring into your eyes, and you would have admitted to any heinous crime.

Too little eye contact suggests a lack of strength or purpose. We have all talked to someone who wouldn't look us in the eye and come away feeling cheated, having no respect for that person.

If the gaze moves away too quickly we are also concerned, because the person is "shifty-eyed." I was talking to a reporter for a local TV station about a recent mayoral election. One of the candidates, a man running for office for the first time, hadn't learned to ignore the camera. When he was interviewed, he kept shifting his eyes from the reporter to the bright lights and whirring sound. After the interview, the reporter suggested he look at one or the other in the future, because the video was going to show him as a shifty-eyed politician. Unfortunately, there weren't any more interviews before the candidate lost in a landslide.

It is also disconcerting to talk to someone whose eyes are unfocused. This gives a confused, bubbleheaded look to any face.

Excessive blinking and eye watering are other negative signs. Blinking makes us look nervous, and watery eyes make us seem overemotional or weak. Many contact lens wearers don't realize the real NVC price of their lenses, as they rub their eyes in discomfort or wipe away the tears with the ever present Kleenex. Other wearers adopt the "contact stare," blinking only when necessary. Often this gives the face a strained, inflexible look, with the eyes locked open like a Shields and Yarnell robot.

Make certain the windows to your soul aren't clouded, giving the wrong information to the people in your life who are looking in. Practice civil inattention with *everybody* no matter what a person's physical condition. Look people in the eye as you listen, and don't be afraid to look away as you talk. It's normal. Keep your eyes on your subject, and your attention will follow.

Nose

Some people can make a career out of a nose, like Jimmy Durante, Bob Hope, and Cyrano de Bergerac. To most of us, the best nose is one people don't notice. There are all types of noses: hawkish curved noses, pixie upturned noses, sharp pointed noses, flat boxer's noses, and noble Roman noses. Each of these is a stereotype that helps affects your image regardless of your real personality. Some people find the stereotype so distasteful that they modify their noses. Most of us are content with what we have.

There is really very little to "read" about a nose other than the nostrils. We can be likened to rabbits, nostrils quivering in anticipation, or racehorses, nostrils flared with eagerness. Often we widen our nostrils in fear or anger. Nostrils can provide some information, but why should we pay attention to them with what is waiting below?

Lips

Lips are one of the really interesting parts of the body. Humorist Richard Armour devoted an entire essay to Sophia Loren's lower lip.

Lips are often linked to aggression. "I'm going to give you a busted lip!" "Don't give me any of that lip!" "Why don't you keep your trap shut?"

We even judge character from lips. Lips can be full or thin. Full lips make people look softer, warmer, and more sensual. Thin-lipped women frequently apply their lipstick outside of the lip line to give them a more sensual look. People with thin lips, such as Jack Lord in the original TV version of *Hawaii Five-O*, show more strength, firmness, coldness, and less emotion. Who wants to let a career depend on a tight-lipped manager?

Children often thrust their lower lips out in angry defiance. Grown-up lips can pout with petulance or sneer with superiority. Lips can also drool with idiocy, part with promise, smirk with certainty, be bitten with nervousness, be licked with worry or anticipation, and have a host of other interesting movements not particularly pertinent to a business book. One of the most common things they do is smile.

Smiling frequency is a learned cultural trait. People in some areas of the country, primarily the South, smile more than others. Studies have shown that Atlanta, Memphis, Nashville, and Louisville residents smile the most. Where do people smile the least? No surprise here—according to research, it is New York City.

Every face has a *resting position*. This is the expression we have when our face is in "neutral," not showing any spontaneous or controlled emotion. (This is not a poker face, when we are trying to mask our feelings.) As we work, a large amount of time our face is expressionless (or so we think).

Some people have a built-in smile or frown at the corners of their mouths. A vertical line at the lip corners also gives the impression of smiling frequently. As the customer from Chapter 1 who covered his mouth when listening knew, heavy facial lines running from the nose to the edge of the lips give a deep frown. All these resting positions affect how we look to others in our unguarded moments.

As you walk outside or around your building during lunch hour, start watching the faces of the people you pass. You may be surprised to find that the majority have a frowning face resting position. The ones with a truly neutral look or the ones with pleasant expressions will appear much more friendly and warm. Which one are you?

Chin

The chin is often considered an indicator of personal strength. Whenever we have problems we have to "take it on the chin." Westerns are full of square-jawed heroes teaming up with lantern-jawed ex-sheriffs to stop those cowardly jowly outlaws.

"Faced" with the big gunfight, the old-timer pats us on the shoulder and tells us, "Keep your chin up, kid. These varmits will scatter at the first shot!"

We stroke our chin thoughtfully and reply, "Quit jawing at me, pops. I ain't scared." Sticking our jaw out defiantly, we stride off towards the fateful showdown.

This whole important exchange would never have been possible without that wonderful device that holds our lower set of teeth. The point is, the shape and position of the jaw contribute to our image.

Square or angular jawlines are associated with strength. Rounded jawlines are associated with warmth and openness. John Wayne, Clint Eastwood, and Kirk Douglas all show strength. Dick van Patton, Dom DeLuise, and Jim Gaffigan appear more open and people-oriented. Jacqueline Kennedy Onassis showed an angular strength, while Shirley Booth showed her warmth.

The jutting chin can create an aggressive, defiant look. The receding chin connotes meekness or lack of character in people's minds. It is such a negative factor that it is often used for comic effect.

The skin around the chin is also important. Loose, jowly skin under and around the chin softens the personality and can even suggest weakness. Former Senator Sam Ervin's chin reinforced his easygoing slow-country-lawyer image. On women, this feature often contributes to a warm, grandmotherly image.

In general, the chin is not an item you can "read" for personality information. Instead, you should be aware of how the chin contributes to your image and the impressions you get from others.

Skin

One of the most common things skin does is get red, or blush. This uncontrollable burst of color across our face is a dead giveaway when we are embarrassed or self-conscious. In general, the easier we blush, the less strength and authority we appear to have. This is unfortunate, since blushing is largely an uncontrollable event, usually aggravated by some noxious co-worker who loves the power of being able to visibly embarrass someone. There is no way to "poker face" a blush. We immediately let other people know they have scored.

In addition to color, our skin shows physical depth and firmness. Thin-skinned people, literally and emotionally, appear sensitive, gentle. You have to approach them with finesse and care. Thick-skinned people are tough, in control, and hearty. You can be more direct with them, more open and blunt. They admire forceful, aggressive people. It's tougher to "get under their skin."

Our skin can appear firm and tight or soft and droopy. Romantic literature is full of phrases such as "skin stretched tautly over high cheekbones beneath intense eyes" or "bulbous cheeks bouncing hideously as he tore at the turkey leg." Much like the loose skin around the chin, loose facial skin projects a softer personality. Firm skin connotes strength and, taken to the extreme, can indicate a nervous temperament.

Wrinkles are another frequent negative. An article in a December, 1977 issue of the *St. Louis Post-Dispatch*, noted that President Jimmy Carter had wrinkled considerably since his election. The comments ran from Vice President Walter Mondale's "I wish he had more time to completely relax" to Atlanta lawyer Charles Kirbo's "I think he is aging." Commonly thought of as one of the hardest-working Presidents in recent years, Carter was described in the article as "an American executive with workaholic tendencies."

The photo on the left in Figure 4–4 shows President Carter during the campaign. The photo on the right shows him in office. The new look Carter was said to have "strain ... etched in his face and around his eyes." Although the lighting is different in the two pictures, in the later photo the President's brow is furrowed, and there are deeper valleys around the eyes and mouth and loose flesh under the chin. This important change in image may hurt President Carter unfairly, since the article also points out that the President's physician pronounced him "in better health than when he entered the White House." His exceptional longevity and vitality are a testament to that.

Figure 4–4. President Carter's wrinkles.
(Wide World Photos)

Hairstyles and Accessories

Hairstyles can play an important role in shaping people's image. John Molloy recommends that men wear their hair like the men in authority they deal with, and that women wear neat styles of medium length without excessive wave or curl.

For example, men calling on executives who wear short hair should also wear their hair short. Don't be like long-haired comedian Ricky Jay, who observed, "I perform for people who have spent their entire lives working to earn enough money to get away from people who look like me."

This works in reverse too. A friend of mine who is a reservist, and thus has to wear his hair short, worked as a salesman calling on head shops (retail stores specializing in drug paraphernalia). Even though he wore appropriate clothes (jeans), store owners were reluctant to trust him and buy from him. He finally had to buy a wig in order to fit in.

In general for men, the shorter the hair, the more conservative the look. For women, the longer the hair, the more feminine the look. The shorter the style, the more conservative. Hair color can also contribute to people's image. While blonds may have more fun socially, brunettes are considered more authoritative.

Baldness frequently makes a man look more powerful and authoritative. Look at Mr. Clean, Kojak, Daddy Warbucks, and Yul Brynner in *The King and I*. Total baldness is best for showing power. The effect is lost somewhat when there is a halo of hair on the sides, or when side hair is combed over the bald spot.

A toupee can have a mixed effect. First, it is an obvious show of vanity in a man, something America's "wooden Indian" concept of masculinity looks down on. It also can be a bad toupee. I remember seeing a graying man with a toupee in a restaurant. He looked like he was carrying a puppy on his head, because the toupee was the color of his long-lost brown hair with the gray showing at the bottom.

Sometimes a man will not be consistent in wearing his toupee. You may see him wearing it one day and several weeks later walk by a bald man without recognizing him. Consequently, the toupee becomes a source of distraction. On the positive side, a toupee is well worth the investment if the improvement in self-image causes a change in behavior for the better.

Facial hair also affects a man's image. One secretary told me that ever since the 1972 Olympics, every young executive she sees looks like Mark Spitz. A mustache can make a young man look older, but it has a price. It is very difficult to counteract the natural frown a mustache gives a face, much like the painted frown on a circus clown. The farther away the viewer is, the less the lips appear to be smiling. If the mustache is too long, lunches can get very messy. It's difficult to be impressive with a drop of hamburger grease beading on your upper lip hair. A mustache that is too large, such as a handlebar or Pancho Villa style, can also detract from a man's professional appearance.

Chin hair is OK today, but it should at least be neatly trimmed. A businessman wants to look dignified, like Sebastian Cabot, not shaggy, like Hopalong Cassidy's sidekick Gabby Hayes. Goatees are fine, but not so much scraggly chin whiskers.

At this writing, sideburns are supposedly going out after their time in the sun. I'm not sure they were ever in, considering the way top executives have ignored hairstyles. I may be prejudiced against sideburns, because I can't grow any (I just don't have the follicles.) Still, I believe they fall under the category of detractors. The best sideburns are those that when asked of someone, "How long were his sideburns?" you reply, "I don't know. I never noticed." Most men don't want to look like Elvis, nor do they want to have a Little Rascals bowl cut.

Whatever your hairstyle, you should look neat at all times.

There is no reason not to stop in a restroom before any important meeting to make an appearance check, particularly after lunch. Comedian Shelley Berman tells of coming home from an unfriendly date one evening to find a piece of spinach plastered on his front tooth. Going directly to any meeting after walking around outside gives us a disheveled non-professional look. Don't let it happen to you!

For those of you who are as blind as I am, glasses are a major head accessory. Although you may feel like you are looking at life through two toilet paper rolls, others observe your glasses as part of your image. In general, glasses make people appear more studious and can help give a face authority. This advantage can be reduced, though, if you wear glasses with oversized lenses, flashy colored frames, or those designer glasses with distracting initials on the frame.

I wear wire rims, and was told when I was younger that they make me look older. (Now that I'm older, they are effective at hiding the bags under my eyes!)

For men, heavy plastic or horn rims can have the same studious effect (although they don't provide as big a field of vision.) Glasses can be an asset for women because they often create a more businesslike and authoritative image. Fashion frames or greatly over-sized lenses will undo this advantage, as will half-glasses worn down the nose in the "granny" or "grandpa" look.

So on the body movement scan, notice a person's head position and features. The position and expression will give you an indication of how people feel about themselves and others. And the hairstyle and accessories will help you analyze their images.

Posture

Posture is very closely related to the center. Stooping closes off the center. And pulling the shoulders back makes the center aggressive.

Stooped or bowed shoulders can mean many things, all negative. You may be burdened, self-conscious, unconfident, submissive, beaten, guilty, or afraid.

Retracted shoulders may make you appear insensitive, angry, impulsive, belligerent, domineering, or mean on the negative side. Depending on your other scan signs, you may also appear forceful, confident, firm, tenacious, and authoritative.

Raised shoulders usually show tension or even apprehension and fear. Squared shoulders generally suggest strength and responsibility.

Have you ever caught yourself driving home from work with your shoulders hunched up around your ears? You probably thought, "I didn't realize I was this tense. I think I'll relax."

You drive along a little farther and reflect, "Gee, that worked once. I wonder if it will work again?" So you relax your shoulders a little more.

I have driven home from a tough sales day and done that four different times. Each time I thought I was fully relaxed at last, but with the tension of the day and of the evening rush-hour traffic, I couldn't relax all at once. Many of us spend a good deal of our day in this posture, transmitting our worry and tension to the entire office with our shoulders.

Leaning is another facet of posture. The way people lean often indicates how they feel about others. Generally, leaning backward is negative and leaning forward is positive. ("I'm leaning toward a free trade agreement.")

When juicy gossip hits the lunchroom table, you can see people lean forward with interest. You go into your boss's office to ask for a raise, and the boss leans back in the chair in a superior position to listen silently as you talk.

Leaning affects height relationships. When we lean backward, we gain artificial height might because we are now looking down at others, even if they are standing and we are sitting. If we lean forward, we pass the advantage to others or at least neutralize it, because we are level or looking up at them.

There is at least one advantage to leaning forward. I recently had a press release photograph taken for use with my seminars and articles. The photographer suggested I lean forward, looking the camera directly in the lens with head erect. Interestingly, the pose gave me a more aggressive appearance.

Seating postures are also important. In general, the more relaxed we are when sitting, the higher our status. This made it easy for Joe B. in Chapter 1 to pick out the Star and Heel in any group. We would never think of going into our boss's office, plopping down in the chair beside the desk in a comfortable slump, and saying, "Howya doin', super cheese?" The boss could easily do this to us, though.

Superiority is also shown by relaxed postures such as feet on the desk (if it's your desk, the boss is crowding your territorial space and showing contempt for your possessions), tilting back in the chair with hands behind head and legs crossed straight out in front, or sitting on your desk (crowding your personal space along with a height advantage), or sitting turned with a leg over the arm of the chair.

Your sense of presence and authority can also be increased by having what my portrait photographer called a "solid base." He told me that too many PR pictures are posed so that the subject looks like an anvil sitting on a TV tray. He positioned me in a chair turned just slightly away from the camera with my elbows out and hands placed midway down my thighs. This way, my figure was narrowest at the head, angled down to the shoulders, and then angled wider below the shoulders because of the arm position. No part of the background showed through under the arms to spoil the base. A courtroom judge benefits from this look because of the flowing robe. Any clothing of this type—a toga, a dashiki, or a flowing evening gown—adds to our image by solidifying our posture.

Hands

There are four basic areas of the hand: tips, palm, edge, and back.

Hand motions involving tips are usually emphatic, as in "making a point." We discipline our children by shaking our finger at them or poking them in the chest. As we turn to leave, they shoot us in the back with the index-finger barrel of their "handgun" smoking in their imagination. At the Cotton Bowl in Texas, fans cheer their Longhorns using the famous "hook 'em horns" gesture, with index finger and little finger extended. Uncle Sam looks us in the eye, points his finger, and emphatically lets us know, "I want YOU!"

Showing the palm is a friendly, peaceful motion. Historians speculate that it originated when people extended their hands on meeting to show they had no weapons. At a church altar, celebrants extend their arms, turning palms out, and intone, "Go in peace, the service is ended." The rock star acknowledges the cheers of the youthful crowd by waving hands overhead with palms out. We wave in greeting. The Indian greets us with steady palm out. The *Star Trek* writers gave Mr. Spock the Vulcan version of the ancient Hebrew greeting with second and third fingers parted.

Edge-of-hand gestures are very forceful, like karate chops. They add sharp, quick bursts of punctuation to our movements. We thrust away a thought we disagree with. We strike the table with the edge of our clenched fist. We use the edge of our hand much like a sword, slicing horizontally and vertically to defend or attack.

The back of the hand shows vitality. It can be aggressive, unfriendly, or negative. The forceful edge-of-hand fist salute becomes "shaking your fist" at someone just by turning the hand so that the back is facing outward.

Nelson Rockefeller showed us the older generation can learn from the young when a photographer caught him with his middle finger thrust defiantly upward at hecklers. The same gesture is not nearly offensive enough if it is given palm out. Try it in a mirror and see. In Britain Churchill's victory sign, known the world over, becomes the equivalent of our one-finger salute if it is shown with the back of the hand outward. We express disbelief by touching our fingertips to our chest and saying, "Who me?"...all back-of-hand gestures.

A closed fist is the universal sign of force. It is rarely positive in a business environment, where it can signal anger, disagreement, fear, frustration, or power. We often employ a fist for emphasis, using it to pound our palm, pound the desk, or pound the other person.

A modified version of this requires wearing a ring. An evening student of mine who is on active duty with the Army told me about certain officers known as "ring pounders." These are service academy graduates who seem to develop the habit of pounding the flat of their hand, the one with the graduation ring, on the desk as they speak. It is irritating to the team, but helps the officers dominate any meeting they are in.

The service academy ring is a good example of using jewelry to advantage. In general, any hand jewelry other than wedding band and watch can be detrimental to your gestures.

Any jewelry that makes noise, such as a bracelet, is reason for justifiable homicide by your fellow workers. One day with a jangling bracelet wearer is enough to make you want to lop off both his or her hands. Your watch should fit your wrist snugly, so that it doesn't bang around.

Married travelers may think they are clever by taking off their wedding ring for business trips, but most single people I know have learned to look at the ring finger carefully. If it has had a ring on it regularly, the finger will show an indentation.

In general, distracting or noisy jewelry should be kept to a minimum. It will most likely detract from your business image rather than add to it.

Legs

Although we spend a large amount of our business time sitting, we also have to stand and communicate, if only at the water cooler.

A wide stance with feet spread apart is very powerful. We can picture a coach coming out, stopping with a wide base, putting hands on hips, and yelling, "Everybody in the pool!"

A narrow stance is weaker. Imagine the coach coming out, putting hands on his hips with feet in the dainty model's T, and suggesting, "Okay, now, let's jump in that pool!" It just doesn't play the same.

We can also interpret how people position their legs when sitting. In almost every tense situation, such as an appraisal or a job interview, a man will cross his ankles in front of him. A woman will usually cross them under the chair. Crossed ankles are a readiness sign, showing self-control.

Crossed legs, on the other hand, are a sign of unreadiness, or non-concurrence. For women, this means the leg-over-leg position. For men, it's the ankle-on-opposite-knee or "figure 4" position. For some unknown reason, we rarely make a decision when one foot is off the floor. It's something that salespeople are trained to notice.

A special case of leg position is walking. Are you a wall hugger? Then you probably create the impression of being shy and diffident, because you are giving ground and making it easier for others to pass.

Aggressive, dominant people walk down the middle of the hallway, making others edge to the side to pass by. If they come face-to-face with someone, they stop and make the other person step aside so they can pass.

Many NYC experts read too much into walking. One book claims that a springy, bouncy walk shows enthusiasm and a high energy level. I normally walk this way, but there are many days I'm not too enthusiastic. In my case, I was a high-jumper in college, and I just have a naturally bouncy step regardless of how I'm feeling. Essentially, if we walk with our eyes and center, the feet will follow. The first two indicators are more important than the feet.

Women and men who wear high-heeled or platform shoes should realize what they are doing to themselves and their walk. It makes for an awkward-looking gait.

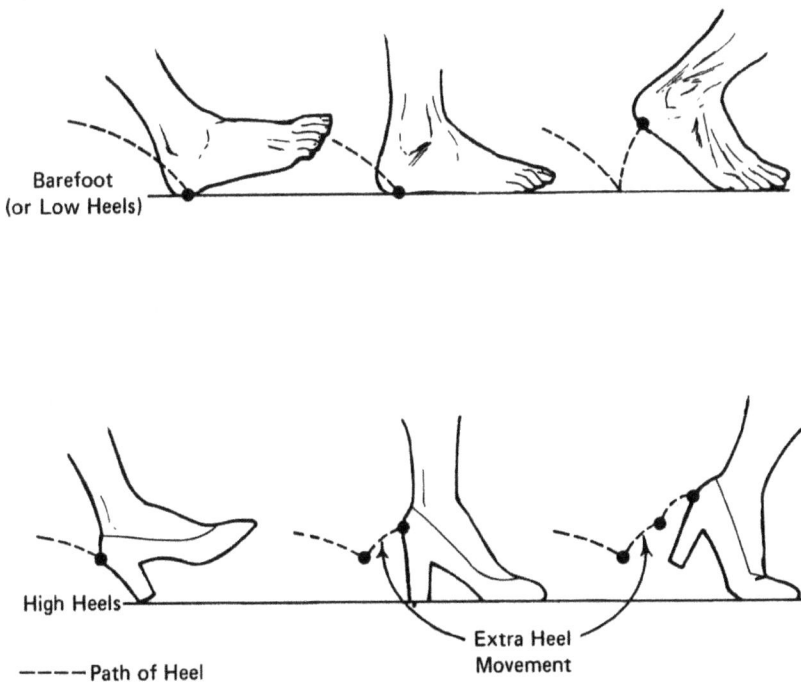

Figure 4–5. High-heeled walking.

There is a reason why their walk is so clunky, and why they have to take little steps. It is because high heels force an unnatural motion of the heel. Look at Figure 4–5, showing a bare foot stepping down. When the heel touches the floor, it does not move until after the foot has rotated flat. The heel finally rises off the ground as the weight is shifted forward for the next step.

With a high-heeled shoe, the foot must continue to move after the shoe heel touches the floor because of its distance from the ground. As the foot rotates flat, the heel moves forward up to two inches for a three-inch heel. The heel then rises normally for the next step. The only way to reduce the extra two-inch arc is to take smaller steps and come down nearly flatfooted, causing the clunky high-heeled walk. There is no way to walk normally in high heels. For image reasons alone (ignoring the ankle injuries), extremely high heels can negatively impact your image.

Summary
This chapter introduced the third NVC checklist, one that helps you evaluate body features and movements. As you observe others, ask yourself:

1. Are people open or closed, aggressive or submissive? (CENTER)
2. What do their head positions, facial expressions, and features show? (HEAD)
3. How do they hold themselves? (POSTURE)
4. What type of gestures are they using? (HANDS)
5. What are their feet doing? (LEGS)

You now have the information you need to systematically read and evaluate someone's NVC. With practice, you can quickly scan body location, surroundings, and body features and movements head-to-toe. You can also begin to better control your own NVC to improve your business image. To be fully prepared for this, you next need to take a more detailed look at gestures.

CHAPTER 5

Interpreting Gestures

ARMS AND HANDS ARE second only to the face in expressiveness. They can tell stories in a hula dance or transmit detailed speech to the deaf. They can provoke a fight or start a crowd screaming or laughing. They can summon the waiter with a check or control a postgame traffic jam.

Many vocations have special gestures. When I was a rod man on a survey crew during the summers, I learned a complete set of hand signals from the transit man (walkie-talkies were not popular then.) If I was not holding the rod vertical, he would put both hands over his head, palms together and lean in the direction he wanted me to straighten the rod. If I was laying stakes off line, he would point to the side I should move. The faster his arm pointed and returned to his side, the smaller the distance I should move.

Deep-sea diving, an environment where speech is useless, also has a gesture language for standard or expected situations. Thumbs up or down means ascend or descend. You point in the horizontal direction you wish to go. If you point to your watch, you are indicating it is time to surface because of dwindling air supply. If you point to your compass, you are asking, "Which way next?" A hand extended palm up means, "What next?" Emergency signals include clutching your neck, running your hand knifelike across your throat, removing your mouthpiece, and pointing to your regulator.

Standard Gestures

Standard social gestures are called *emblems*. The hitchhiker stands at the roadside shaking an extended first with thumb out. If something is satisfactory, we signal okay by putting our thumb and index finger together in a circle. The peace sign is given with palm out and index and second finger extended. For a time, the peace sign was a greeting signal between the young, replacing the wave or handshake.

It seems like every winning football squad on New Year's Day runs off the field with index fingers proclaiming, "We're No. 1." We indicate other numbers by raising the proper number of fingers. If the number is higher than five, we open and close the hand for the proper multiple of five and give the partial hand count at the end.

We also have gestures that show pictures. I always ask for the check at a restaurant by catching the eye of the waiter and drawing a square in the air with my finger. I have never had this sign misinterpreted. We may diagram a football play on our hand or describe the route to our office by tracing the directions on the desk.

I once appeared in a silent movie to be used as a coffee break film at a large regional computer sales meeting. An associate of mine played Charlie Chaplin's Little Tramp, long before that image was use in a national ad campaign, and I played a typical young salesman in the early 1900s.

One scene called for us to watch an old-time card sorter in action. At the last minute, we were unable to come up with an old enough machine, so we played the scene in pantomime. I walked up to an empty space and proudly pointed out the machine with a wave of my hand. Then I carefully removed the imaginary large cover and folded it up. I gave a brief silent explanation of the various parts of the machine and loaded in the cards.

We were worried that the sophisticated business audience wouldn't accept this bit of make-believe. It turned out the gestures were more than sufficient to capture the audience's imagination, even reinforcing the silent movie feel, and the film was one of the highlights of the meeting.

Other standard gestures show space relationships. The most common is the fish story. The erstwhile Captain Ahab describes his battle with a Maybe Big Fish, arms getting farther apart with each retelling. We can't seem to keep from giving space relationships even if we are talking about the near miss in the parking lot, or coming "this close" (holding finger and thumb two inches apart) to blowing up at a subordinate.

When I tell my classes about my encounter with Mike, the man with no intimate space, from Chapter 2, I always hold up my hand with thumb and little finger extended saying, "This far" to indicate how close our faces were. Then to make it come alive, I then pick out some poor unfortunate, put my thumb to my nose, and move up until my little finger is almost touching the subject's nose.

We often use gestures to mimic others. A successful insurance agent I know sells seemingly on raw instinct. There is little relationship between his approach and any information the potential client gives him. Still, he has an uncanny success rate of calls to sales.

As we were talking about this one night, I asked him to describe his last sales call that day. As he talked about the sequence of events, he began to unconsciously act out the parts. I was seeing a stage version of his sales call. He was able to notice and use the NVC the clients gave him. But better yet, he remembered their actions and could apply them in later calls. As the night wore on, I realized that he had to recreate the movements of each customer to be able to tell me about the sale.

We all are natural mimics to some extent. Otherwise, we would never have learned to walk or talk. You can watch two people from across the office and often tell what they are talking about by their movements. The storyteller will "conduct" the story in addition to telling it, sometimes performing the solo parts, too.

Gestures can be used to trace the flow of a discussion or to list the main points of an argument. We summarize a conversation where we give both points of view with an open palm turned upward ("On the one hand...on the other...") The opposing points are counted on the fingers of each hand. We can even tell which side a person is defending by the hand that is used. A right-handed person usually reserves the favored point of view for the right hand. The reverse is true for the left-hander.

You can tell which hand a person usually uses by the watch or fitness tracker. Except for the small percentage of left-handers, most people wear their watch on the left hand, a fact that has kept mystery writers in plot clues for years.

Touching

We reveal how we feel in many situations by how we touch ourselves and others. Some touching gestures are important indicators. Others are mannerisms that have outlived their usefulness.

Rich Little, one of the few comedians to "do" Johnny Carson, talked about how hard it was to develop his Carson impression. Watching Carson's monologues for several shows, Little counted over 20 self-touching mannerisms that were part of Carson's regular delivery—smoothing the coat, touching the face with index finger, straightening the tie, and so on. Although many of these gestures are associated with nervousness, Carson claimed that he was not really nervous. He made the gestures because he was keyed up for each monologue.

I became aware of two unconscious mannerisms of mine when I went out for track in college. Because the frames of my glasses interfered with my vision when I high-jumped, I switched to contacts for workouts and meets. During practice, I found myself jabbing my forehead between my eyebrows with my middle finger. I also put my hand over my face and grabbed my temples with my thumb and ring finger. I kept wondering why I was doing this, and I'm sure the other jumpers were scratching their heads, too. It finally occurred to me that I was pushing up my nonexistent glasses. I had gotten into the habit of doing it habitually, and my brain had not figured out yet that I was not wearing glasses.

We all have these useless little mannerisms. I'm more aware of some of mine because my college students frequently use me as the subject of their NVC term project. I wipe chalk off my clean hands, push my glasses up my nose, rub the skin on my left hand where a steel splinter resided for several years, and more. I can only hope none of these mannerisms is too distracting to my classes.

My students, however, know how to "drive me up a wall," sometimes purposely. My favorite villains are pen-clickers, pencil tappers, plastic food wrap fondlers, head scratchers, and face contortionists.

One double-jointed student used to absent-mindedly bend her index finger *backward* and touch the back of her hand. It made my hands ache to watch.

Touching other people is a complex mannerism in our society. A study of conversations in outdoor cafes in several countries confirmed our reserved British heritage. Four cities were observed for touches (self and others) per hour of conversation. The results were San Juan, 180 per hour; Paris, 110 per hour; Gainesville, Florida, 2 per hour; and London, 0 per hour.

Touching is restricted in our society because certain areas of the body, on ourselves or others, are considered taboo. In the early years of television, married couples portrayed on TV weren't even allowed to sleep in the same bed. Greetings were confined to gentle busses on the cheek when the husband came home from work. Today there is a just a bit more realism in the way married people are portrayed.

In a social or business setting with friends, certain portions of the body are touchable. The order of the most acceptable to least acceptable areas for women are hands and forearms, upper arms and top of head, head and shoulders and feet, and finally torso and legs. For men it is hands, shoulders and arms, top of head and upper body and legs, and finally lower body.

Every woman has experienced an unwanted male hand creepily resting softly on her shoulder. Many men have also encountered female associates whose constant touching makes them feel uncomfortable.

With strangers, we prefer no touching whatsoever. Notice how salesclerks will jerk their hand back if they accidentally touch a customer's hand while returning change. Observe how people will stand as far apart as possible on a crowded bus or elevator, shrinking back from each other even as they are forced together (public space.) Unwanted touching is the ultimate indignity to territorial space needs.

Professionally, the only universally acceptable touching at work is a handshake. I've seen a deal killed by a hearty back-slap afterwards.

Many people touch objects in a habitual fashion. The number of chewed pencils in offices would embarrass the beaver population. We chew the ears on our glasses and nibble on toothpicks, letter openers, or cuticles and fingernails when we can sneak them. I am always amazed by the number of people I see chomping away on their fingernails as they drive home from work. Mangled fingernails, a tribute to our high-pressure work world, may be the first symptom of ulcers.

Capitalizing on this need to handle something other than ourselves or our associates, fondle factories have produced a variety of touchables. If Captain Queeg can have his marbles, executives can have their paperweights, trophies, toy awards, doodle pads, Rube Goldberg phone directories, and giant erasers. (Ever notice how the giant erasers get dirty long before they are even slightly used?) One reason jewelry is so popular is that it has a high fondle value. Twirling a bracelet or ring is satisfying and reassuring.

All these touching signs in our culture are good indicators that a person is seeking reassurance. They can also hint at nervousness, insecurity, lack of self-confidence, impatience, or fear.

Gestures and Emotions

Consistent with the idea that you are looking for a correlated read using multiple NVC signals, the same is true for linking gestures to perceived emotional state. Gestures tend to come in *clusters* by major emotion. Here are some examples.

Anticipation

One of the most common gestures of anticipation is the open palm of someone expecting a tip. Rather than regarding a tip as an act of appreciation, they turn it into a bribe to make them leave before guilt or irritation overwhelms us.

Waiters often use a more subtle approach. They probably get shorted as frequently as anyone who lives on tips, but they are much more civil. They linger by your table as you get up, so that if you don't leave a tip, you know that they know it.

Another sign of anticipation is the prayer hand position, with palms rubbing back and forth as if to roll out a piece of dough. Without this typical gesture, arch villain Snidely Whiplash could have been played by R2D2. No self-respecting villain would ever snatch even the most insignificant deed out of the freezing widow's grasp without a little gleeful hand rubbing.

Diners sometimes make this gesture as they first sight and smell their meal. In a meeting, some executives will "tip their hand" by making this gesture when they are about to jump on a mistake. During a sales presentation, I saw that one of the managers was going to break in with just such a point, so I stopped and said to his boss, who had a puzzled look, "You had a question?" By the time the boss was done, the manager's point was no longer pertinent and somewhat off the subject.

Anticipation also tends to increase the number and speed of our movements. The rhythm of people's gestures is tied to their speech patterns and emotional state. We need to become aware of any changes in this rhythm. A small child will jump up and down with excitement waiting in line for Santa. A teenager will run up and down the stairs and dart from bathroom to bedroom getting ready for that first date. Two parents may pace, fidget, or get into an argument waiting at the airport for their child to return home from a military deployment.

There are other, more superficial signs of anticipation. We cross our fingers to express hope (originally an early Christian religious sign) or to protect us from lying. We hold our hands together in prayer and look upward for guidance. We "knock on wood" to ward off any bad luck in mentioning how good life has been or what misfortune we have avoided.

A sharp intake of breath often indicates anticipation. The karate expert prepares for a blow with a sharp breath and shout. Spectators at the circus collectively breathe in as a difficult trick is begun, letting out a large "Oooooh" when it is completed. To this day I find myself taking an anticipatory breath when I see a child sassing a parent, because in my childhood this was always followed by a quick shot to a spot inducing temporary pain.

Stress
The nonverbal signs of stress are closely related to those of frustration, anger, and worry. Stress gestures often involve the fist: hands in fists at sides, crossed arms with fists, fists resting on a desk, banging the table with a fist. (The child's version is arm waving.)

Clenched hands, a modified fist gesture, is also a sign of anxiety. Pictures of disaster survivors grieving for their lost friends or relatives frequently show the subjects in this position. It is almost as if we need to hang on to someone or something, even if it is ourselves in times of stress.

Another stress gesture is hand wringing. One TV advertisement for an office copier was designed to promote the portability of a particular model. The star of the ad talked to us as if we were in the office with him. He pointed out a feature of the copier and then turned away to explain it to us. Behind his back, someone rolled the copier off for other uses. When the actor turned back to the machine and realized it was missing, he made the typical hand-wringing gesture of anxiety. Turning back to the camera, he bumbled out of control until the person returned the machine.

We frequently show stress by rubbing the back of our neck, called *defensive beating*. A popular oil filter commercial features a smug service station mechanic pointing derisively at some poor yuk who is trudging to his car with an obviously large garage bill in hand.

The mechanic says something like, "See this little thing? It costs about $5.00. He could have bought one of these and saved himself that big bill. You see, you can pay me now or you can pay me later."

The effective part of the commercial is the actor in the background. He walks out to the car rubbing his neck like he's just pulled a muscle, looking at the bill and shaking his head. He gets in the car and just sits there, defensively beating himself until the commercial is over.

An experienced bartender reported to one researcher that the defensive beating gesture was a good indicator of a potential fight. The fights were usually started by the defensive beater.

Many signs of worry or stress involve self-touching. A common one is rubbing the forehead, usually done with thumb on the cheekbone and the first and second finger on the forehead, as if rubbing away the worry lines. It also hints that we have a headache from all the problems.

We often rub at our eyes, pull our cheeks, and generally rub our faces in a series of beaten exhaustion moves. We may even stretch slowly and rub parts of our body to psychologically wipe away the strain of the problem.

We also sigh a lot. Without the sigh, those John-and-Marsha daytime serial actors and actresses would be nearly mute.

(Sigh) "John, darling, I don't know what we're going to tell Randolph about the results of the tests."

(Sigh) "Marsha, he must be told before Penelope gets to him about the affair."

(Sigh) "Penelope wouldn't do that, would she?"

(Sigh) "You know she's always hated us, Marsha."

(Sigh) "I guess we do deserve it, after testifying about her addiction to mint cookies at her incompetency trial."

The sigh says, "Listen to me. I have something more than air to get off my chest." It slows down the conversation; it gives dramatic pause. It gives us a chance to glaze over pained expressions and worried brows without the distraction of words. The sigh often says, "I'm under stress."

Skepticism

Closing off the center is a common indicator of skepticism, suspicion, or secretiveness. Arms crossed tightly over the chest or crossed casually on the desk signal a potential communications problem.

Suspects being interrogated by the police frequently use their folded arms to help "clam up," closing their center (and mouth) as tight as a clam shell. A variation in a non-intimidating situation is to put one or both hands over your mouth, as if to say, "Speak no evil."

Scratching the face is another sign of skepticism. Comedian Bob Newhart started his career playing the skeptic in a number of unusual situations, such as being the watchman on the Empire State Building the night King Kong scaled it, being a game manufacturer the day Abner Doubleday called up to talk about baseball, and being a marketing adviser when inventor Herman Hollerith called to introduce his new punched-card sorter. Newhart's standard "You've got to be kidding" gesture is scratching underneath the eye with the middle finger. Some people also pinch the bridge of the nose, as if to say, "I don't believe this!"

We reject ideas by waving them away with a palm-out swipe from side to side as if to say, "Go on!" We use the hand in imitation of the head shake to say, "No, no, no" in a back-and-forth erasing motion.

Psychologists theorize that the negative head shake is a relic from infancy when we nursed at the breast or bottle. When we were not hungry, we rejected the nipple by turning the head sharply to the side. Since I have never found a baby willing to talk about it (don't blame me, I've tried), I'm a bit skeptical of this interpretation. I believe that it is another cultural trait learned by imitation. For example, a parent wags a finger at a naughty child. Soon the child is wagging *his* finger at his dog or his friends.

Nervousness

We have to move when we get too nervous. A theater audience begins to fidget when one of the characters is about to make a fool of himself. A co-worker tells us she just "can't sit still today." Something is moving all the time in nervous people. Their fingers drum the table. They tap their pencil. They doodle, or they tear paper into little pieces. I remember one customer who used to rub the stickum off transparent tape. (This is not an easy process, as any accomplished tape rubber will attest.)

Many people are incessant coin or key jinglers, or constantly fiddle with their jewelry. They are unaware of their actions, or else they surely would stop. Even ignoring the noise, it's an annoying nervous habit.

I occasionally fall into it, too. To fight its effects, I keep my right pocket (I'm right-handed) empty of everything but my handkerchief. My coins and keys are in my left pocket. Since the pockets seem so irresistible, I have developed the habit of putting only my right hand in my pocket, which is also easier on the suits. Since there is nothing to play with other than a no-fun cloth, my hand stays fairly idle and my pocket-plunging needs are satisfied.

You can fight nervousness by keeping your mouth busy. Anna in *The King and I,* found that whistling helped her fight nervousness and fear. Whistling, like yawning, seems to be a community affair. If one person in an office starts whistling, by lunchtime the whole organization sounds like a magpie convention during a spontaneous rally for their favorite bird.

We tend to do a lot of self-repair when we are nervous. Scientists call this *preening*, named after the action of birds that smooth their feathers. We tug at our skirt or pants. We brush at our hair with our hand or straighten our belt or tie. The more we do this and the longer it lasts, the more nervous we are. For example, I have seen some job seekers preen through an entire 30-minute interview.

Self-Assurance and Superiority

One of the most condescending and irritating signs of self-assurance I have ever seen involved sports. When Red Auerbach was head coach of the Boston Celtics basketball team, he had a habit of lighting up a cigar when he felt victory was assured. The earlier he did this in the game, the more insulting he was to his opponent. The crowd and the announcers picked up on it and made it that much more noticeable. Nothing could have been more irritating to an opposing player than to see Auerbach smugly puffing his victory stogie.

Placing the hands above the shoulders, is another superiority gesture, especially when you raise them over your head, The boxer traditionally clenches his hands aloft. The President acknowledges the cheers of the crowd by waving both hands over his head. The football team chants, "We're No. 1" with hands up in the air, index fingers pointing to the sky.

A confident executive sitting in an office may lean back and talk with hands clasped behind his head. This gesture is always a part of a relaxed posture, which, as noted in Chapter 4, usually connotes higher status. The center is very open, almost aggressively open, with the hands in this position.

Psychologists theorize that we raise our hands over our head to raise our height—that this series of gestures is tied to height might. This may be true, but many other self-assurance and superiority gestures don't require increased height.

One of the most common is *steepling*. The high steepling position is to have the hands with opposite fingertips touching (like a "spider doing pushups on a mirror") and fingers spread widely in the shape of a spired church. The elbows are usually on the table, so that the center is somewhat closed and the hands are up around the face. The index finger and/or thumbs may be touching the face.

Medium steepling has the elbows on the table, arms in a 45 degree position, with hands clasped, perhaps with the index finger extended.

Low steepling is when the forearms are on the table, or in the lap, with hands clasped.

Many businesspeople realize that showing superiority through steepling is not necessarily good communications, but unconsciously engage in it anyway out of habit.

Hands on hips is another common self-assurance gesture. The Jolly Green Giant towers ominously over his valley standing with legs spread and hands on hips, booming his benevolent, "Ho, ho, ho!" Mr. Clean gets rid of dirt and grime and grease in just a minute and, incidentally, stands around with hands on his hips. Parents will confront their wayward child by standing with hands on hips, in effect saying, "And what do you think *you're* doing?"

The strongest form of this gesture is to have the fists on the hips. The next strongest is to have the hands open and pointing downward, thumbs on one side of the hips and fingers on the other. Hands in pockets or thumbs looped into the top of pants or the belt loops are weaker versions.

Hands behind the back is also a self-assurance gesture used by leaders. The Army drill instructor strides purposefully in front of the green recruits, chest thrust out, arms clasped behind his or her back. The teacher tells students how poorly they have done on the midterm exam, hands clasped behind, shifting back and forth from the heels to the balls of the feet.

Insults and Anger

Consistent with human nature, our gesture vocabulary is full of insults. The most common is one mentioned earlier, the "finger" (or the "bird,") where the middle finger only is extended from the fist and displayed at our target. It is a very taunting gesture, suitable for someone who has just driven us off the road, heckled at our speech, insulted us, or made off with our date.

Next on the insult list is the gesture made by placing your left fist with palm down on your upper arm near the elbow and bringing the other arm up into a "shaking your fist" position—the "up yours" gesture.

If you need a more socially acceptable gesture, "thumbing your nose" has a certain poetry to it, as you put your thumb on your nose and waggle your fingers in derision.

If noise is what you need, the Bronx cheer can show it with a wet "Blthblthblth" (just put your tongue between your lips and blow).

If it's disrespect you're looking for, flapping your ears could be the answer. In imitation of donkey ears, you put a thumb in each ear and wave your fingers.

If you don't like to get your chin wet with the Bronx cheer, you can at least stick out your tongue.

In a role-playing session recently with a large group of students, I played an argumentative employee and they took turns acting as my manager. When I logically backed one poor student into a corner and countered her last point, she finally crossed her arms in desperation, got a very determined look on her face, and stuck her tongue out at me. After the class and I stopped laughing, I teased her about breaking role and she replied, "Who broke role?"

We like to insult someone's intelligence by letting them know we think a "screw is loose" or there's "nobody home." The first we do by rotating the index finger near the temple. The second, by tapping the temple with the finger. We make the cuckoo sign (the brain is supposedly going round and round) by circling an index finger around our ear.

Sometimes we roll our eyes and look skyward, as if to say, "Oh, Lord, why me?" A Xerox commercial that has run several seasons shows a monk who is told to make several hundred copies of an excruciatingly detailed handwritten manuscript. The enterprising monk sneaks off to his local copy center and comes back with copies the same day. When he presents them to his superior, who in awe mumbles, "It's a miracle!" the young monk rolls his eyes and looks off in disbelief at the superior's ignorance.

Another insulting gesture is the thumbs-down movement, used to reject another person or idea. This gesture can be traced to ancient Rome, where it was used in audience surveys, only in the opposite way. When a gladiator was defeated in combat in the arena, the victor had the option of sparing him or killing him on the spot. The spectators could signal life or death by holding out their fists with the thumb pointing downward, meaning to lay down the sword and spare him.

Today we give the thumbs-down sign as negative feedback, like when someone else is talking and we want to indicate our disagreement without speaking. Thumbs down becomes an NVC "Kill it!" or "It'll never get off the ground, Orville."

As mentioned in Chapter 4, most gestures indicating anger are back-of-hand movements. Giving someone "the back of your hand" is one. Shaking your fist is another.

Finger pointing and chest poking can also indicate anger, although they are closely tied to frustration. You begin pointing a finger for emphasis in a conversation only when you feel that you aren't getting your point across or that the person is not listening. The more the person argues, the more aggressively you point.

Another indication of anger is not moving at all. You make no gestures as you talk or listen. This anger sign usually elicits the comment, "Is there something wrong?"

A teacher will stop talking and stand motionless until a whispering student notices that nothing else is going on in the room. A subordinate will sit frozen during the critical part of an appraisal as the boss details the subordinate's shortcomings for the year. Other versions of this are the "silent treatment" and the "cold shoulder." The lack of NVC signs becomes an NVC signal in and of itself!

Summary

You've had the chance to learn some of the standard gestures for showing emotions. Since many of these integrate several parts of the body, they were examined in what researchers call "gesture clusters." In the next chapter, you will learn NVC behavior clusters for a variety of common business situations. By understanding your environment and making maximum use of NVC in these situations, you can increase your ability to communicate successfully in the business world.

CHAPTER 6

NVC in the Office

THERE ARE A NUMBER of common business situations where you can exercise your new knowledge of NVC. Some, like riding in an elevator, are merely fun to experiment with. Others, like meeting someone in an interview, can help you communicate better.

The Elevator Syndrome

It never ceases to amaze me that the most dynamic people in the world become shy and awkward on the elevator. Riding an elevator has to be one of the most uncomfortable events of our day. Because of this, there is a complete set of unwritten rules in elevator behavior.

When you walk in, you punch the proper button, move to the nearest open spot, and turn to face the front. All conversation must stop. You probably pull out your phone and look at it. As more people get in, you shuffle over (nobody ever walks or takes steps inside an elevator) to make room, preferably not touching anyone.

If you must touch someone, you keep your body stiff and unmoving at all times as if to say, "Uh, I'm not getting any pleasure out of touching you."

As the elevator empties, you again shuffle to recreate the even spaces between you and the other occupants. If you are in back and need to get out, you mumble, "Out, please" or "'Scuse me" deferentially. At no time do you look anywhere but at the lighted numbers above the door or at the top of the button panel.

I can see the UFO training instructor getting ready for a close encounter of the third kind: "Today, class, we are going to study the archaic human up-and-down box. Now remember, the first rule is no gronkling."

A slow student pipes up innocently, "But don't these poor beasts wish to share their discomfort by communicating with each other in their little box?"

"I can see you still don't understand the primitive human animal, Thyroid. It's true that humans crowd themselves into winged transportation devices, pack themselves into a dark room to watch projected images, or attend a sports contest and scream with thousands of their own kind. But they really don't like to be together. It makes little sense, I know, but that's what you've got to keep in mind if you want to pass."

Poor Thyroid didn't realize that the elevator is really an NVC nightmare. All those strangers are shoved into intimate spaces. Sometimes they even are forced to touch. There is no place to morally rest their gaze. And since they are together for such a short time, they have no chance to transform themselves from non-people to real people.

There are a number of different approaches to this discomfort. Some people walk on and stand right in front of the button panel. They are out of the way of the door with their backs to a wall where they won't be forced to move as the car fills and empties. Though everyone entering the car has to reach around them to punch a floor button, they maintain the "panel position."

Others go straight to the back of the elevator and lean against the rail, even if they are getting off at the next floor.

Still others prefer to travel the elevator in pairs, much like people in a restaurant going to the bathroom in tandem. They wait until someone else they know is elevator-bound and then walk on together. Their conversation dies as they enter, and then restarts in mid-sentence as they depart.

What all these people would really like to do is to walk straight to the back of the car, stand facing the wall about six inches away, and over their shoulder say, "Somebody tell me when we get to the fifteenth floor." Then they wouldn't have to interact with anyone.

You can experiment with your new knowledge of NVC the next time you ride an elevator. Pick a spot somewhat off to the side (but away from the walls) and don't move as the car fills and empties. This will throw everyone's territorial space gyrations out of kilter. If you end up on the same side with the only other occupant, see how he or she reacts.

Or if you have the fortitude, get on a crowded elevator, push your button, then face the crowd, looking everyone in the eyes. One executive likes to get on the elevator, face the occupants, and jovially say, "You may wonder why I called this meeting," looking everyone in the eye. Try it.

Another behavior that makes us uncomfortable in an elevator is loud talking. Mustering your courage one day, get on your elevator and boom to the crowd, "Howya all doin' today? Nice weather we're having, isn't it? How many came in on Highway 40 today?"

When nothing happens, say, "C'mon, let's see a show of hands." If you still get no response, start asking them one-by-one, "Do you drive to work?" This is really fun in the morning when everybody is grumpy and half-awake anyway.

I had an opportunity to experiment with elevator NVC when I was a salesman. My company was located on floors 8, 9, and 10 of our fifteen-story building. Employees were always going a short hop up or down while the other building tenants were going the full trip to or from the lobby. A salesman named Jim and I started a quick-thinking game involving weird questions. The idea was to try and stump the other person speechless, or have them break up first.

One day, as I was riding up to 10 from the lobby and Jim got on at 8, our conversation went something like this:

"Jim! When did they let you out of jail?"

Not batting an eye, he said, "Oh, the lawyer posted bail in about two hours."

"Did they ever find the gun?" I continued.

"Not yet," he said.

"But what did her father say?" and the elevator doors opened at the tenth floor.

We walked off leaving a carful of people leaning after us as the doors swished closed.

The point is that everyone pretends not to listen on an elevator. But of course, they really are listening. I like to think that Jim and I brightened the lives of many of our fellow travelers.

Greeting Behavior

Part of the problem in an elevator is that we don't have the time to properly greet one another. We have probably all ridden the elevator hundreds of times with people who work on nearby floors without ever meeting or greeting them.

The first stage of a greeting is *orientation*.

I once was walking down the hall at one of my major customer's offices when I passed a man who looked very familiar. I must have looked familiar to him too, because we both had a puzzled look on our faces as we passed. We had noticed each other, and were in that uncertain area where you don't know whether to say "Hello" and risk feeling foolish or to ignore the other person and risk being insulting. When we were about fifteen feet past each other, we both turned simultaneously to look back.

When he exclaimed, "Ken!" his name came to me. It was a personnel executive I had talked to six months earlier about putting on a seminar for his division. We laughed about acting in unison in our mutual confusion. We had both noticed each other but had been trapped in indecision over whether we should greet.

When the executive turned, I saw the second stage of greeting—the *eyebrow flash*.

After you orient your eyes to someone, your eyebrows tend to move sharply upward. If there is a delay in recognition, there will be a double flash as your eyebrows first move up in recognition, then move further up in greeting. Try it some time with someone. Just double-flash your eyebrows—nothing else—and see what happens. The other person will almost always take that alone as a greeting.

The third stage of greeting is the *salutation*.

It is always a good idea to include a person's name in your salutation. Repeating the name helps you remember it the next time you meet. It is also music to your friend's ears. We all love to hear our name. You can hardly say it too much.

Have you ever gone up to someone you thought you knew from behind, tapped her on the shoulder, and said, "Hi, Rita!" only to have her turn around and be someone else? As you slink away looking like a mobile red stoplight, you vow never to make that mistake again.

You can take advantage of an NVC sign called "name sensitivity" to avoid such cases of mistaken identity. Go up behind the person and quietly say his or her name. People are especially attuned to hearing their name. If you get any physical reaction out of your target, you know you have the right person and can continue in safety. If you have the wrong person, they usually never even heard what you said.

The fourth stage of greeting is *presenting the palm*.

We can do this with a wave. You can wave your whole hand at the wrist by rotating your forearm. Or you can wave by holding your hand up and bending only the fingers or by moving the fingers independently in a ripple motion.

If you are close enough for contact, the universally acceptable business greeting is the handshake. The hand extension for the shake should be well timed. I have seen two people do the "quick-draw boogie" as one put his hand out too early and withdrew it just as the other person extended her hand. The longer your hand is extended ungrasped, the greater your embarrassment and insult. But someone needs to go first. Make that you.

Your handshake is a large part of the first impression you create. Pity the people with cold or naturally sweaty hands, for they have a strike against them. (Breathing on your hand or wiping your hand on your pants or skirt before you shake only makes matters worse.)

It sounds trivial, but when I was a salesman, I always wore a warm pair of gloves in winter so my hands didn't feel like ice cubes when I greeted a prospect. I also made it a habit to keep my right hand out of my pocket and to carry my leather attaché case in my left hand to avoid a sweaty handshake. If I had to dry my hand before ending a call, I tried to do it unobtrusively a few minutes before wrapping up.

The pressure of a handshake is also important. We have all shaken hands with the "dead fish" and wanted to buy back our introduction. One of the engineers in my office had this type of handshake. Although he was a strong, beefy guy, his handshake was wet toast. When I mentioned it to him, he explained that he had accidentally injured some people when shaking hands. A good "rule of thumb" is to match the pressure used by the person you are shaking hands with.

The politician's handshake, offering the hand in an L-shape so that only the fingers can be grasped, is poor in business. You should always offer your full hand to someone, unless you are meeting a macho limb crusher. If a crusher gets your knuckles in his grip, you are maimed. One option is to thrust your hand fully into his so that your knuckles are past his grip, and then hope for an early parole.

The last stage of proper greeting is *eye contact*.

Most of us have been taught to maintain strong eye contact as we meet—to look the other person in the eye and not look back down until we are seated and into our conversation. Wrong! When you meet people, especially for the first time, always give them a few seconds to look at you unobserved so they can form that necessary first impression.

For example, I have asked executives what they look for first in a job candidate. While there is no consensus, you hear things such as hair length, clothing, pants crease, shoeshine, etc. The learning point isn't what these hiring managers looked for. It's that they all looked for *something* when sizing up prospective employees.

You need to give the people you meet that opportunity to get their preferred first impression in a comfortable fashion, without having to sneak looks throughout the conversation. One way to do this is to provide each person you meet with two or three seconds of unobserved eye contact directly after the handshake.

In my sales calls, I always did this deliberately. After shaking hands, I would look away, turn to put my coat down, lay my briefcase out, take the chair facing the person, sit down, grab whatever papers I needed, and finally look up. Although this took only a few seconds, it gave my customer enough time to check me out in comfort. For a short period, I experimented with skipping this part of the greeting. But I could sense the difference in the early stages of sales calls. So I went back to providing the short eye break after the greeting.

We have different approaches in greeting people at distances. When we see a friend coming toward us on the street or down a long office corridor, we quickly look down and keep walking until the person is about ten feet away. Then, as if on cue, we look up in unison, exchange greetings, and then look back down as we pass. (It always amazes me when I see high-level executives walking with their eyes at their feet.) We have to look down because the other person is too far away for us to continuously look at as we approach without violating moral looking time.

Just for fun, the next time you are walking along and see acquaintances down the hall coming at you, look at them and greet them the entire time. Keep smiling and waving as you approach. It will drive them crazy.

Or try the opposite approach, which tends to happen all the time in an office. Look up too late for a mutual greeting. Keep looking down until you are abreast or the other person, and then quickly look up as they pass and say "Hello." You will be past them and heading away before they have a chance to respond.

You know what you're thinking when that happens to you. "Should I say go back to hello to him?" or "Will she think I snubbed her?"

The point is not to make all your co-workers uncomfortable. It's to understand the proper spacing, the unwritten rules, to greet people as you move through your office.

There are other times when we wish to pass through a group without stopping to make any contact. Sociologists call this *territorial passage*.

The most obvious sign that people want to avoid communicating is lack of eye contact. They will pass through the group with their eyes down, mumbling, "Excuse me" or "Pardon me." Their hands will frequently be held down or in front of the body, further showing their desire to pass unnoticed.

If someone wishes to join the group, he or she will attempt to move into the circle of discussion. If the group expands and the members open up their centers, the newcomer will maintain heavy eye contact with the speaker and group members and eventually take a verbal "turn."

Conversation

Taking a verbal turn isn't always as easy as it sounds. We have all been in a situation where we "couldn't get a word in edgewise." Worse yet, we've been trapped in a conversation, forced to sit there nodding our head like one of those annoying little dolls in the rear window of an automobile. A student told of being at a gathering with a tipsy drinker who was a nonstop talker. Being polite, the student wasted nearly two hours trying to get away from this marathon mouth.

Other people have a habit of interrupting frequently. One of the hardest lessons for a sales trainee is learning when the customer is finished talking. I had one particularly slow-moving (and slow-thinking) customer who would insert long, reflective pauses into our conversations. At first, I assumed he was done and immediately responded to his comments. He would patiently wait for me to finish and then continue where he left off, ignoring everything I had just said. This customer still holds my world's record for the longest pause in the middle of a conversation—60 seconds. Yes, he once sat for a full minute before continuing with his next sentence! In crowds, he is relatively quiet because no one is willing to wait that long for the next thought to drop.

It is simple to determine when someone is done talking. We tend to mark the end of our speeches with physical signals. We look down or away when we are done, breaking eye contact and control of the conversation. Many times a change in posture will accompany the change in speakers, called a "postural shift."

On a recent vacation, I saw good examples of this in the hotel lobby. The tours operating from the hotel required the guests to be out of their rooms by noon on the day of departure. Since the planes did not leave until five in the evening, the lobby was full of guests killing time. Almost as if they had all read the same book, the individual conversations were carefully marked. As one man stopped talking, settling back as he looked away, his companion would lean forward to begin talking. As she finished, she would turn slightly and cross her legs for her listening stint.

When people are not done talking, they will hold their postural position. They will not look down, or away and down. They will keep their head and hands up to show a desire to continue.

If they are in a group, they may use sounds to maintain control of the conversation. Sounds like "er," "uh," and "ah" keep sounds coming out as people gather their thoughts, and force others to appear to be interrupting.

Another way to "hold the floor" is to look up and away during pauses. I always joke that there must be a fascinating painting at the point where the wall and ceiling meet in every room because people look there so much. If you want to make a dramatic, reflective pause in your conversation without being interrupted, the wall-ceiling glance is your good bet. Accompanied by a little thoughtful chin rubbing, it will turn you into a surefire intellectual.

Listeners will signal when they want to make a comment to take over the conversation, usually by assuming an erect readiness posture and giving a fast series of agreement nods.

Figure 6–1 shows a manager with his administrative assistant. In the top picture, the manager is talking. In the bottom picture, the admin is responding.

Figure 6–1. Conversation body positions.

Notice that when the manager is speaking, he sits as close to the desk as possible and leans forward. He has a slight smile on his face and is palming with one hand. His other hand rests relaxed on the desk. He appears to have a very careful, controlled nature. His coat is still on, and the papers on his desk are neatly arranged in rows. He is obviously right-handed, with his coffee cup, phone, and pens all lying to his right. The office is in the normal back-to-wall arrangement. The admin is sitting in a relaxed posture. Her arms are crossed in a modified closed center, and her legs are crossed casually.

In the lower picture, where the admin is speaking, things are reversed. The admin has uncrossed her legs and arms, moved forward in the chair, and assumed an upright posture. One leg is tucked under her chair in a readiness or alertness position. Her chin is tilted up. The manager has assumed an open listening position. His arms are resting comfortably on his chair. He has pushed away from the desk and is leaning back in a superiority posture. His chin has dropped, indicating that he has stopped speaking, but he has not brought his head into a submissive position. His head remains level, a very open sign.

It is almost like a conversational dance between two people. One moves forward to speak, then sits back to listen while the other person moves forward to speak—back and forth in rhythm.

In your own conversations, watch for the NVC signs that act as traffic signals for the discussion. If you don't see a marker such as a postural shift, dropped head, or eye contact, stay quiet. The other person isn't done. Otherwise, your partner will signal you when he or she is finished speaking.

There are also a number of NVC signs that indicate whether you are really getting through when you talk.

In a good conversation, both parties will often assume the same body position. One salesman in my office did this so often in the casual bull sessions on the sales floor that I couldn't resist trying a small experiment. We started talking at my desk, which was next to a window. When I sat on my desk, he sat on the desk too. I casually moved over to the window and he followed, keeping his normal personal space. I sat on the heater module, tucking one leg under me, and he did the same. I stood up, and within one or two sentences he stood up. He was always not just in tune with others, but physically in tune, too. The point is, we all signal a deep level of communication by mirroring the body positions of those we are speaking to.

Another good indicator of successful conversation is something called *resonance*.

We all tend to move synchronously with someone we are listening to. When the top picture in Figure 6–1 was taken, the admin was bobbing her crossed leg in time to the boss's right-handed gesture. Sometimes we nod our head in time to a speaker's movements, as if to say, "I agree" or "I understand." We may drum our fingers in time to the pacing of an instructor or sway to the music of a film presentation.

Resonance is also an indicator of relative status. Whoever controls the tempo of the movements is usually the higher-status person, or the NVC leader. If you notice yourself resonating with someone else, change the tempo and see if the other person follows. If you observe two people resonating in a conversation, watch who begins a pattern and who follows, then see if that agrees with your perception of their status relationship.

Instructing and Presenting

Instructing or making presentations is a special type of conversation. People who treat instruction as a one-way communication process are making the mistake of communicating "to" instead of "with" their audience. Sometimes people end up communicating the wrong information, which can detract from their real message.

I once ran into this problem in one of my seminars on professional growth. Midway through the morning, a woman sitting in the front row farthest to my left began to giggle. Fearing the worst, I paused and asked her, "OK, I know I'm missing something important. What's going on?"

She managed to choke out, "You have a safety pin in your rear." As you can imagine, then entire class burst out laughing.

I knew at once what had happened. In a class the previous week, I had accidentally sat down on a piece of fluorescent pink chalk. When my wife took the pants to the cleaners, they had evidently put a safety pin on the stain. There are certain things you can't do and be cool, and patting your rear in search of a safety pin in front of 30 strangers is one of them.

I made a similar gaffe recently just before I was to give an early morning body language speech to a large group of computer salespeople. The meeting was held locally, so I merely had to rise early and drive to the hotel across town. But being a true night person, I felt like a 45 rpm record being played at 33-1/3.

After asking only three people how to find the headquarters meeting room, I walked in to greet my contact. He introduced me to all the people in the room—two women and four men—and then took me to his boss. I remember thinking they were a particularly friendly and cheerful bunch for such an early time of the day, a nice group. My contact suddenly got a strange look on his face and then asked, "Would you like to go to the cafeteria for a cup of coffee?"

Not sensing the urgency in his voice, I replied, "No, thanks, I'm not a coffee drinker."

His boss broke in and said, "Then why don't we walk on over and take a look at the auditorium where you'll be speaking? I'm sure you want to get comfortable with the facilities." As we walked over, he quietly said, "Your fly is down."

Now, every man has been caught by this joke dozens of times in his life. The secret is not to panic and clutch your crotch. To be on the safe side, I said, laughing, "This is why I carry a briefcase," and held my leather folio in front of my waist. I took a few more steps thinking, "Why would he pull this one on me?"

As I brushed my fingers over the top of my zipper, I noticed a distinct separation. (That jaunt in from the car had seemed kind of cold.) I had just walked through a crowded lobby and met some members of my meeting group, fly flapping and white jockey shorts winking brightly through the gap.

Trying to salvage some measure of self-respect after being the body language expert who showed up opened up, I mentioned the old flying joke, "Well, my brother the pilot instructor told me you should never fly if you're the type of pilot who walks out of the bathroom with your zipper down. I guess that's me."

When that was rewarded with a sincere chuckle, I thanked the boss, "Charlie, I appreciate your not letting me go up there like this." He wondered if I did it on purpose, but I reassured him that there were more professional ways to make points on appearance. It was just a standard case of brain cramp.

Appearance is critical in any group communications session. Think of either of these two stories before you rush into a meeting. No matter how late you are, there is always time for a quick 360-degree turn in front of a mirror to spot any irregularities that will destroy your image and change initial respect into derision.

Good Presentation NVC

Chapter 2 discussed the importance of laying out a room to give an audience comfortable personal space. One of the problems with many presentations is that there is often too much distance between the presenter and the audience. In a small conference room holding 20 to 25 people, the lectern may be as far as 15 feet from the first row of chairs. If the attendees, like most people, tend to hang back then the distance is even greater.

I always move the lectern closer to the group whenever possible. When I can work without notes, I stand as close as possible to the audience without invading the social territorial space of the people in the front row. This has several advantages.

First, the audience is more controllable at close range. The farther away you are, the easier it is for an audience to whisper, doodle, or doze off. The increased distance gives them a false sense of invisibility.

Height advantage is also diminished with distance. If there is an interruption, it is much more difficult to regain your listeners' attention if they are 15 feet away.

Finally, your voice may not be able to carry to the rear rows of listeners. It is not enough to be heard by those in back. You must be heard throughout your full range of speaking to be effective.

It is often helpful to actually "get into" your group during a presentation. At an advanced business seminar that I attended at Harvard Business School, one of the professors used this technique. He literally ran up and down the aisles getting close to people who wanted to make a comment or ask a question. Although the students were initially amused by the professor's antics, they paid more attention to him than to any other speaker in the series. The course was also much more informal and relaxed.

You can also create a more casual atmosphere by keeping your center open. I never say a word to a formal group with my coat buttoned, nor do I ever wear a vest to a talk or presentation. Whenever possible, I remove my coat. I do not loosen my tie in a business setting, because I believe it looks sloppy. The loose-tie image is better for after 5:00 P.M. when you are trying to convince your boss that you're working too hard.

A problem that many speakers have involves eye contact. As mentioned in Chapter 4, people normally maintain eye contact less than 50 percent of the time when speaking. In addressing a group, the presenter must break this rule dramatically, maintaining eye contact with somebody nearly 100 percent of the time. This total eye contact can be extremely uncomfortable.

Many instructors try to solve the problem by looking only at one student, seeing the audience as a blurred sea of impersonal faces, or not looking at the audience at all. Some presenters pick a spot slightly above everyone's head in the back of the room and watch it as they talk. This gives the same distracted effect as a TV personality reading teleprompted lines just off camera.

You must develop an *audience scan* technique. The goal is to make all the members of the group feel as if you have looked at them personally during the talk. If you let your eyes sweep across the audience, you are not really making any eye contact, because it falls below the time that is required for making individual connections.

Instead, your gaze must jump from person to person, resting on each one for at least moral looking time. Anything less is ineffective. Anything more is intimidating.

With this scan, you have to be doubly conscious of the edges of the group—front and back, left and right. If your eye jumps in a back-and-forth, left-to-right and up-to-back pattern, you will be looking at the edges only half as much as the middle. This is particularly true of the front corners. Edges get only one look per sweep. The middle gets two looks each back-and-forth sweep.

I find that simply scanning randomly and concentrating on hitting the edges more often is sufficient to help me maintain better eye contact. I don't follow a specific pattern because I'm afraid to look like a searchlight in the night. This random pattern works effectively for very large groups too, because you can hit more people with a single jump. At a distance of 50 feet, 15 or 20 people will all think you are looking at them individually.

At times you may want to intimidate an unruly listener. A silent, piercing gaze will direct the group's attention to the offender. We've all been talking to someone during a meeting and suddenly noticed that the room was quiet with everyone looking at us. Or found that the speaker is focused solely on us.

There is also a rule about gestures in presenting: *make some.*

Many speakers cling to the lectern like a life raft. If the speaker ever lets go, he or she will drown. The presenter starts with both hands gripping the sides of the lectern. As the speaker moves to the left, the right hand lets go and grabs the left side before the left hand lets go. The process is reversed in moving to the right. Occasionally, the speaker may daringly let go and make a feeble move with one hand before vertigo sets in and the errant hand returns to its permanent roost.

In addition to making gestures, unlock yourself from the lectern. I have found that my listeners are much more responsive when they have a moving target to follow. If you stand in one place, you will lull your listeners into a stupor, similar to highway-stripe hypnosis. People's eyes need to move around in their heads. And their heads need to swivel to keep the brain lubricated. This doesn't mean you have to put on roller skates every time you plan to stand up and say something. But the longer you talk, the more you should provide your audience with a variety of movements for visual stimulation.

When you must stand at the lectern, don't fall into the "Coast Guard sway" shown in Figure 6–2.

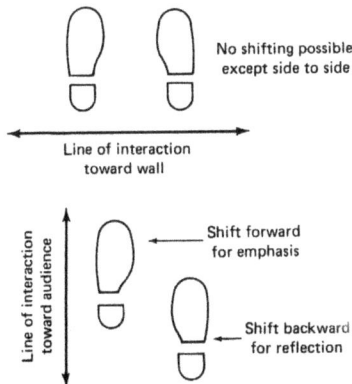

Figure 6–2. Lectern stance.

This is when you tightly grip the lectern on both sides, feet planted widely, and sway left and right toward the side walls as you speak. You had better put Dramamine into the coffee, because the only listeners who won't be seasick in a few minutes are the Coast Guard people.

Interact with your audience rather than along your audience by placing your feet approximately shoulder width apart, and putting one foot slightly in front of the other (your "best foot forward" of course). No side-to-side movement is possible in this position. Instead, this allows you to shift toward the group for emphasis, and away from it for reflection.

Imagine an old-time preacher leaning low over the lectern and shouting, "You're all going to hell!" He leans back suddenly upright and asks reflectively, "What do you think about that?" These techniques can help you make better presentations.

You also need to know when you are succeeding and when you are losing the competition for your audience's attention. I can always tell who hasn't done the homework in my college classes. A student may walk in and claim, "I really liked that Principles of Management book. Yep, I read the first eight chapters and it was so engrossing."

When I glance down at the student's desk, I notice that the book sits there without binding wrinkles from being opened. Then when I ask for volunteers to discuss the chapters, the student goes on an eye contact vacation.

One of the sure signs of a lost audience is when you can't find a volunteer. You are suddenly completely alone. You're invisible. People look down at their papers, pick at their nails, or gaze abstractly into space. I like to just stand there until someone can't take it anymore and looks up out of curiosity. I then have my subject, and make a mental note to figure out what I'm doing wrong.

I also like to make a game of calling on students who have questions before they raise their hand. The NVC signals for "wanting to speak" are about 80 percent reliable. (Occasionally I recognized people who are just about to scratch their heads). There are some anticipatory signals you can look for.

As in conversation, listeners who want to add to the discussion will usually change positions, sitting up alertly as if to say, "I intend to speak when there is a gap." They will start maintaining solid eye contact with the presenter in order to attract attention when their turn arrives. They will make a small gesture. And they will make some kind of noise, such as clearing their throat or saying "er," to verbally get in line behind the current speaker.

Listeners will also signal attentiveness. As noted earlier, this is affected in part by where people sit in a room (see Zones of Attention in Chapter 2). But body position is a much stronger indicator.

The evaluative King Kong head tilt is a very positive sign of attention, as is resonance with the speaker's movements. Hand-to-side-of-face gestures also show evaluation. Examples of these are forefinger on cheek with thumb and second finger on chin, fingers on cheek, fingers stroking chin, or head on fist. We also sometimes fondle objects such as a pipe or glasses in order to buy time to make an evaluation.

Figure 6–3 shows part of a class that has been kept too late. There is only one positive NVC sign among the three students: the woman's evaluative right-hand position. This is negated by her posture. Like the two men, she is leaning away from the instructor. None of the students' centers is particularly open to the speaker, and two are closed off with either hands or crossed legs. All three have very sober, set facial expressions. The man on the left has a level head position with face turned toward the speaker. The woman also has a normal head position, but her head is turned slightly away from the direction of her gaze. The man on the right has a very negative dominant-disagree head position to go with his closed center and leaning posture. Both men are also gesturing with modified steepling (superi-

Figure 6–3. Losing an audience.

ority.) This is clearly a negative group of students who are showing little empathy or agreement with their instructor.

Gestures of boredom or impatience are other signs of losing your audience. I always joke that the best NVC sign that an instructor is "burying" a class is a red spot on a students' foreheads during a break. (The red spot is from resting face down on the table.) A shaking or tapping foot is also a consistent indicator of uninvolvement. Drumming fingers, twiddling thumbs, and doodling are other signals.

The head-in-hand gesture (not to be confused with hand to side of face) is the worst. If the chin is resting in the open palm with the fingers splayed over one cheek, you can be certain the eyelids will begin to flutter soon after.

As much as I hate to see signs of inattention, they have been of great use to me in teaching. I have very little desire to talk to sleeping people. No matter what my lesson schedule is, I'm better off blowing it with several extra breaks than mesmerizing my students in a frantic marathon day. In communicating with an audience, you should make it easier for people to listen to you. And you should "listen" with your eyes for their attentiveness.

Offices and Meeting Rooms

These are public indicators, and they can convey a significant amount of information. It all starts with the primary workplace division, a person's office or workspace.

Office Layouts

As mentioned in Chapter 2, an office is an excellent indicator of its owner's personality. Figure 6–4 shows three views of one of the most unusual offices I have ever seen.

The top picture shows the view from the door. The middle picture shows the view from the plant. And the bottom photograph shows the view from the visitor's chair. This is one of those rare offices with the occupant's back to the door. The executive likes this arrangement because he is "not distracted by people walking past outside the door."

Still, it takes a very confident and self-assured personality to ignore rear fear. It also takes a lot of self-discipline not to become distracted by sounds outside the door.

Figure 6–4. An unusual executive office.

This office is highly individualized. Classical music plays softly in the background. The greenery is not standard company plastic decoration. It is real and has been nurtured with protective concern by the executive himself. The major wall decoration is a *New Yorker* map of the United States, showing all points west of New York City as something akin to the Indian territories. A clock is mounted in prominent view. The shelves display a variety of cards, mementos, and books on many subjects.

The desk is efficiently arranged. In the middle picture, notice the piles of paper in convenient stacks. Necessary tools such as a stapler and staple remover are out on the desk. The pens are neatly laid out directly in front of the executive (to the left of his glasses.) The executive appears organized but extremely busy.

Compare this picture with the office in Figure 6–1. That executive's desk is much less cluttered and much more organized. No utensils are out. No personal effects show except for the nameplate in the front left corner. The shelves and credenza contain only pertinent books and folders. This office is much more impersonal, giving a serious "no frills" approach to business.

Figure 6–5 shows a diagram of the office pictured in Figure 6–4. It indicates several interesting features in addition to the occupant's chair facing away from the door.

First, the office is designed to minimize a visitor's stay if the occupant wishes it. The executive has a small office space to work with and evidently wants to control most of it. The visitor has very little space, being hemmed in by the plant, desk, couch, and end table.

As the bottom picture in Figure 6–4 shows, the plant can get in the way of a conversation across the desk. As in the classic quick shop commercial, the plant and the visitor "can be very friendly."

Although the visitor does not have enough space to feel totally comfortable, the chair is tall enough (and the executive's chair unmodified) so that the visitor is not at a height disadvantage. In fact, this executive often puts himself at a height disadvantage by sitting on the couch to talk to a visitor. In addition to relaxing his guest, this move opens the centers by removing the desk as an obstruction and minimizes the plant's interference. The location of the couch and the executive's willingness to sit "one down" further emphasize his confidence and self-assurance.

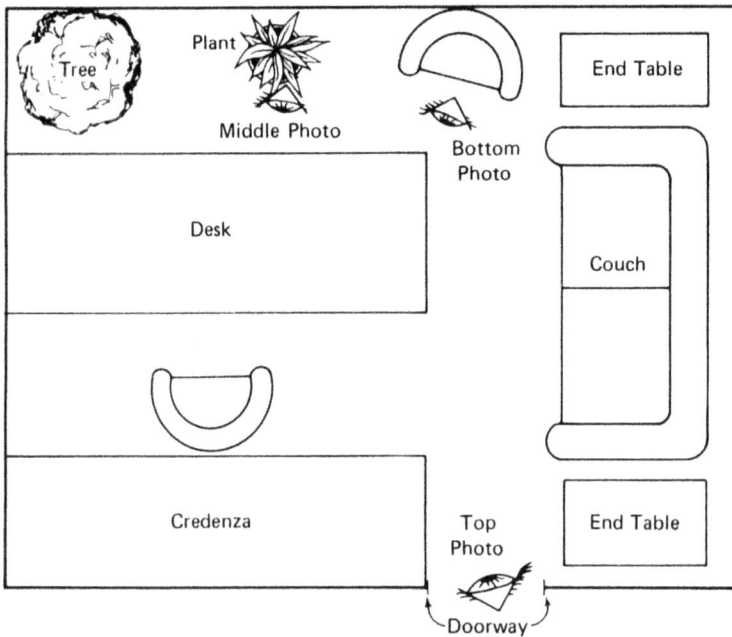

Figure 6–5. Office layout.

Formal Meetings

I recently studied a government agency conference room with a carefully designed arrangement. The diagram in Figure 6–6 gives the basic features.

In this highly structured organization, the seating layout is the basic King Arthur arrangement. At one end of the wide table, the commanding general sits flanked by his chief of staff and deputy. The agency directors sit along the sides in predetermined positions. The greater the director's seniority, the closer he or she sits to the general. Other meeting attendees sit behind the general in six or seven rows of chairs, with special support staff for a particular meeting sitting in the front row. The closer staff members are to the front row, the higher their status.

Those not seated at the table make their presentations at the lecterns. The left lectern is used if there is only one briefer. Both are used if two are speaking. The screen is rear projection, so no audiovisual paraphernalia is exposed. The lighting is uniform, and the heavy drapes over the windows are never opened. The fire door behind the left lectern is always locked from the outside. The main door is behind the rows of chairs, an appropriate distance away from the general's seat to minimize rear fear.

Informal Meetings

Although we may occasionally attend rigidly structured meetings such as those held in a government agency, we can use NVC to better advantage in more informal meetings.

When I was a computer salesman, I discovered quite a lot about one of my customers through a series of informal meetings. The customer

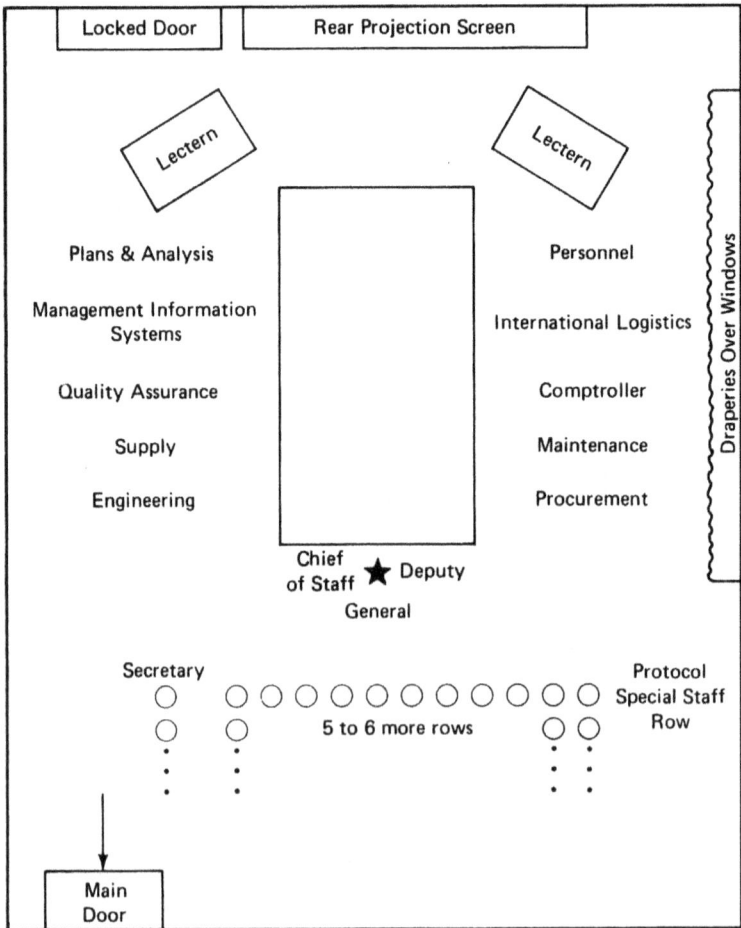

Figure 6–6. Government agency conference room.

had ordered a large computer system upgrade and was having trouble planning and coordinating the physical installation. One of the executives suggested that those involved on both sides begin meeting weekly until the installation was completed.

I was the marketing representative for my company and was accompanied by two systems engineers, a hardware maintenance engineer, and a programming maintenance engineer. The customer's representatives included the programming supervisor, the operations manager, and an operations supervisor. I was responsible for leading and coordinating my company's efforts, but the customer had no single person in charge. In addition, no one had been designated to lead the meeting itself.

When I arrived at the conference room about 15 minutes before the first meeting, I found the customer's programming supervisor already seated at the head of the table, facing the door. It was apparent that he intended to run the meeting. I was content to let that happen and decided to mill around until the meeting started and observe how everyone else reacted.

The conference room was long and narrow, with two tables arranged end to end the length of the room. Approximately ten people could sit on each side. As people filed in, they glanced about the room and, seeing the programming supervisor at the far end, sat down at the other end near the door. I chose a chair in the middle of the group and sat down, fighting a smile. My hunch was that the programming supervisor was very defensive and he might be separated from the others because he was not well liked.

The arrangement was almost comical. There were at least five empty seats between the supervisor and any other person at the meeting. One of the systems engineers walked in late and, looking around in puzzlement, picked a seat midway between the group and the supervisor ("Out of sympathy," he later told me). The funniest moment was when the supervisor began the meeting by saying, "You know, you don't all have to sit down there. I feel all alone." The participants looked at each other expectantly and fidgeted in their chairs, like the contestants on *To Tell the Truth* before the real person stands up. But they all stayed seated. After an embarrassed silence, the supervisor went ahead and began the meeting.

As the weeks wore on, I found that my guess about the supervisor and his relationships had been correct. He was indeed not well liked, and people were resentful of his leadership, even though he was the logical person to run the meeting. He sensed the resentment and bolstered his position by sitting at the head of the table with his back to the wall. The attendees retaliated by keeping their distance. The incredible thing was that we sat like this every week for three months. After the first few meetings, people became accustomed to the arrangement and established their ritual locations.

The lessons to me were clear. Whenever I gave a presentation at the customer's location or wanted to control or lead any type of meeting, I arrived early and claimed the end seat nearest the door. This let the other attendees sit with their backs to the wall. I also pulled chairs at the other end of the room away from the table and pushed them against the wall. I then spaced out the remaining chairs along the table, leaving no chairs at the far end. This forced the attendees to sit closer to me. I learned never to have more chairs at a conference table

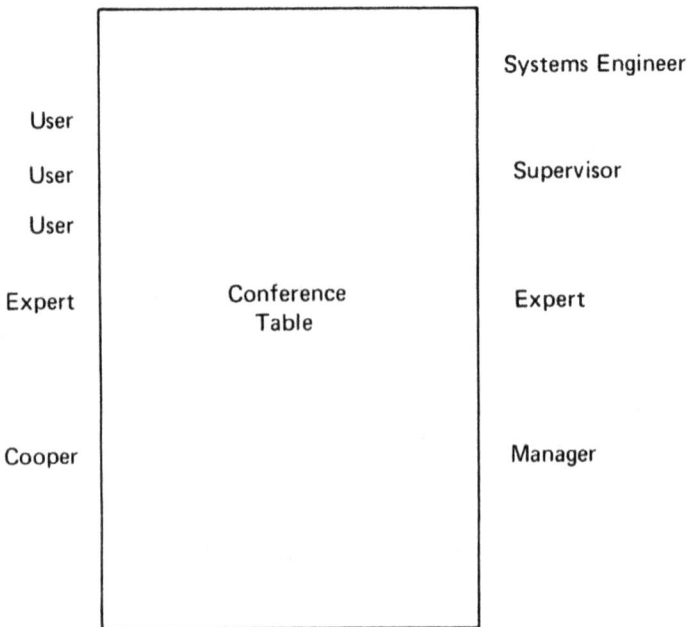

Figure 6-7. Informal meeting.

than I thought I would need, because people will use the ones that give them the most territorial space.

Figure 6–7 is a diagram of another meeting where seating position was important. The meeting was called to market an advanced computer system to appropriate data processing personnel and the potential users of the system.

I brought two experts in from out of town along with my systems engineer. The experts sat down first, across from each other at the middle of the table. The first customer to arrive and sit down was the data processing manager. I sat across from him. Although the programming supervisor and the users worked in different parts of the building, they arrived together and picked the positions shown. The systems engineer then sat next to the supervisor.

This seating arrangement gave me all the information I needed to plan my sales strategy for the meeting. On the basis of what you have read thus far, you should be able to answer the following questions:

1. What was the relationship between the manager and his subordinate, the programming supervisor?
2. What was the relationship between the users and the supervisor? The users and the manager?
3. What role did the manager and I intend to play in the meeting?
4. What role did the systems engineer plan to play?
5. How did the users feel about the proposal?

It was evident that there was no love lost between the programming supervisor and his manager. The supervisor waited until the manager was seated and then chose the one location where it would be almost impossible for him to converse with (or even see) the manager. The three users hovered uncertainly until the supervisor sat down and then sat across from him for easy conversation.

I had no intention of doing anything more than introducing the participants and letting the experts talk to the users. The manager evidently felt the same way, because he too picked a location with little dominance. I later found out he was there just to monitor the meeting and put a stop to any user interest in the marketing presentation.

My systems engineer had been working closely with the supervisor and wanted to help him, but he also wanted to get to know the users better. The users were obviously interested enough to come to the meeting, but they were extremely defensive, particularly toward the manager. They made no effort to interact with the manager, although he was primarily responsible for any projects affecting them. And at no time before, during or after the meeting, did any one user ever get as far as 10 feet from the other two users.

My systems engineer had chosen his seat correctly. If the users were to be influenced, it would have to be through the supervisor, not his boss. I directed the conversation as much as possible to the opposite end of the table, as the systems engineer soon caught on to my strategy and took over.

Afterward, I made it a point to engage the users in a technical conversation until long after the manager had a reason to remain. When he left, I scheduled a follow-up session for the discussions. The two experts were directed to a cab out front, content that they had done their job and oblivious to the wealth of information the meeting had revealed.

In addition to behavior during meetings, it pays to watch how participants mill around before a meeting starts. Figure 6–8 shows a small group talking before an informal departmental meeting.

Figure 6–8. Informal office conversation.

The woman and man on the left are supervisory personnel. Their manager is to the far right, and one of his admins is shown from behind. Notice how both men have modified-aggressive NVC signs versus the women, who are much less aggressive.

The supervisor in the vest is standing with center open, head confidently cocked looking down from a height advantage, one hand in his pocket, with the other arm "claiming" the cabinet, and weight shifted to one leg. The woman on the left is leaning against the cabinet with center partially closed by her posture and low hand clasp, and she is looking up. The admin is standing stiffly with her center closed off by her clasped arms and slightly bent posture. She has her head in a somewhat submissive downward position.

The most important feature of this conversation is the position of the manager. The three subordinates form the corners of an equal-sided triangle with the manager looking in from the outside. Rather than forming a "choir," the group is closed away from him. His neutral facial expression contrasts with the pleasant expressions of the others involved in the conversation. Although he is in a dominant position, with hands in pocket and feet widely planted, he is still formally closed with his leaning stance. If you were dealing with this group, you should be alert for problems. There is something going on between the manager and his team.

Another important feature of the conversation is the difference between the NVC of the two supervisors. While the woman on the left cannot comfortably assume the position of her male counterpart in the vest, she could stand in a more positive manner. She should not emphasize any disadvantages such as height by leaning or slumping.

In Chapter 1 you read the story of Joe B., the architect who could pick out the Star and Heel in any meeting. Figure 6–9 shows a small group listening to a presentation, including two of the people from Figure 6–8.

Using the NVC information you have learned so far, what might this picture be telling you? If we label the participants numbers 1 to 5 from the left...

First, whether intentional or not, there appears to be two groups. That may or may not mean something.

Both #1 and #2 are sitting upright. #1 is attentive, but neutral. #2 seems the more relaxed, with an unbuttoned coat and open center, and is seated at the table's corner. That can connote a power position. His feet are under his chair in a readiness position, and he has an evaluative head tilt.

On the right, #4 is seated between the others, which again may be a power indicator. He also has several negative signs such as crossed arms, a backwards head tilt, chin pulled back, and a backwards lean. Note that his pad is set aside versus being ready for note-taking, and that he is not even wearing his glasses (note the glass case in his coat pocket.)

Figure 6–9. Presentation audience.

#3 seems most interested in the reaction of #4. And #5 is sitting back with a neutral involvement, though his center is closed to the presenter. And the only person with a writing instrument showing is #3.

If you had to pick out Joe B's Star and Heel, you might identify #2 as your star, and #4 as your heel. Again, these are just indicators. But as you can see, you have lots of information to interpret in what, on the surface, seems like a simple scene. You just need to pay attention to it.

Summary

As you have seen, there are many opportunities to use NVC in a business setting. As an instructor or presenter, learn to be the master of your audience. You can control your listeners' receptivity and responsiveness through proper design of the physical layout. You can begin to "read" their reactions to you and your content.

Call on questioners *before* they raise their hands. Make it a goal to never again interrupt anyone, either in a classroom or in a private conversation, by using NVC conversation signals. Learn to enjoy greeting people and be comfortable with the business rituals of greeting.

Use your NVC knowledge of Star and Heel indicators to ferret out your opponents and your supporters in a meeting. Determine what they think about themselves, each other, and you by noting what seating positions they take, whom they gather around them, and what body positions they assume.

View every office as a carefully controlled informal meeting environment that offers even deeper insights into the character of its occupant.

Finally, use what you have learned in this chapter to brighten up at least a small part of your day. Have some fun on that communication torture chamber, the elevator.

CHAPTER 7

NVC and Social Business

I HAD THE OPPORTUNITY to apply NVC under very unusual circumstances several years ago. I was sitting home alone one weekday evening when I received a phone call. It was my wife, who had gone shopping with a friend at the neighborhood market. In an emotional voice she told me that her purse had just been snatched and that she would be home late. She was waiting for the police to arrive to gather all the pertinent facts.

My wife was much angrier when she finally got home. She and her friend had been pushing their carts out to the car when a teenager ran by and yanked my wife's purse off her arm. She did not have a good view of his face as he went by because of the darkness and the suddenness of the theft.

Unthinkingly, she reactively ran after him, only to see him jump in a running car and roar off with two friends. They did not turn their lights on until they were far away, so my wife could not read the license plate. What made my wife angry was that she had absolutely no information to give to the police when they questioned her.

Around 2:00 the next morning, we received a call from a juvenile bureau detective asking us to come down so that my wife could make an identification.

"We've gotten a confession out of one of the accomplices and would like you to identify the one who took your purse," the detective said.

My wife explained that she had no information, but he suggested we come in anyway. As we waited at the station for the lineup to be arranged, I asked several questions about what we were going to do.

In order to be legal, a lineup must place the suspect with at least three other people of the same race and general appearance. It would not have been acceptable, for example, for the young suspect to be lined up with a group of older adults. So the police found three other youngsters for the lineup by putting out a radio call for squad cars to pick up any teenagers fitting the approximate description and bring them in. This point is important in understanding the mental state of the other boys in the lineup.

After talking with the detective, we were ushered into a room where four suspects were standing on a stage with bright lights shining in their eyes. We sat behind a sheer black curtain so we could look at them unobserved. However the identification was going to work it wasn't going to be about clothing. Clearly the suspect had changed clothes since none of the four was dressed like the thief.

The first suspect, a short stubby blond, obviously did not fit the physical description. The other three were similar in overall appearance, and behaved in the following manner:

Suspect #2 was clearly bored and resentful at being put through the inconvenience at 2:00 a.m. when he was "just out minding his own business." He turned insolently when directed, and stood with weight shifted on one leg, hands on hips. His head was tilted back as he rolled his eyes in disgust at each command.

Suspect #3 was very matter of fact. He moved with no hesitation. His face was a relative blank. At the end he stood erect with hands clasped loosely in front of him.

Suspect #4 was totally intimidated by the process, even ashamed. He stood slumped with head down. The detective repeatedly had to tell him to lift his head so we could see his face. The suspect moved in leaden response to each command, squinting in the lights.

We left the room to confer with the detective. My wife told him she could not make a positive identification between #3 and #4. And that she did not want to jeopardize any young man's future with an erroneous ID. The detective then requested that she at least try to make an ID. Even if they couldn't use it in court, it might be useful in interrogation.

DETECTIVE: Could you make a guess as to which one you think it was? We have already have broken down one of his buddies and he knows it. So it could be useful as we question him.

WIFE: Well, if I had to guess, I'd say #4. I really don't remember the thief having a light mustache, but I might have missed it in the dark. Am I right?

ME: No, you're wrong, it had to be #3. (If you're going to stick your neck out, do it with confidence.) #4 couldn't have done it.

DETECTIVE: Yeah, your wife's wrong. It was #3. (Turning to me) Wait a minute, you weren't even there. How did you know who did it?

ME: Oh, I could just tell from their body language.

DETECTIVE: (Walking off rolling his eyes) Oh, brother.

Here is what their body language was saying. What my wife took for guilt in #4 (head down and sunken-in center) was really submission. Here was someone who was obviously ashamed and humiliated at being dragged into a "real police lineup." This wasn't the behavior of a brazen kid who planned the theft and kept lying to police until one of his friends broke under questioning.

But it wasn't really the behavior of #2 or #4 that sealed the deal. The big tipoff was #3's his *lack* of emotion.

#3 was the only one under the lights who wasn't showing *something*. It is natural to have some sort of feeling in such a situation. Everyone should be feeling in some way or another.

You can just imagine what went through his young mind. "I won't show them a thing; I'll be a blank. I'll be a poker face. Then they won't be able to read me."

But everyone else had nothing to hide. So his conspicuous poker NVC was the most telling indicator of all. It made him stand out as the only person up there who wasn't reacting normally to the situation. Then when he unconsciously went into a modified closed center at the end of his movement, clasping his hands low in front of him (the only one to do this), I felt certain that he was the suspect.

I haven't had the opportunity to do any sustained research into the NVC characteristics of suspects in a lineup, but my police officer students always identify the suspect correctly whenever I present this example. In two years I have had only one officer miss it, and that is because he wouldn't play his first hunch and changed his answer. Police officers are adept at reading people's behavior because it's their business. Their lives are often endangered in family disputes where anticipating people's actions can mean the difference between a calming chat and a brawl with family members.

Although picking out guilty suspects may not be a part of your livelihood, there are many other social situations where NVC can be of value. The most common situation is the ritual called courtship.

Courtship Behavior

When two people are interested in each other from a dating standpoint—at work or anywhere else—they may think they are being cool about it, but there are often obvious NVC signs.

I was standing in the noonday line of a downtown burger bar when I saw a fascinating encounter unfold. A young businessman ahead of me, looking to be fresh out of school, was lounging against the wall staring absently into space. An attractive young woman noticed him and walked over to where he stood. As she neared, she called his name and put on a dazzling smile.

He started slightly at the sound of his name, glanced over, and seeing the young woman, proceeded to change in a manner no less dramatic than Clark Kent turning into Superman after a brief visit to a phone booth. As his face displayed the eyebrow flash and smile of greeting, he seemed to grow in height and build before my eyes.

The woman was obviously interested in this young man, for she stood in the classic "total rapture" position—listening to him from a close distance, standing erect with hands at her sides, and looking up directly into his eyes.

They held these positions for several minutes as they conversed in an animated fashion, then the woman turned and went off to her friends farther back in line. The young businessman watched her go with a smile, then slowly reversed his dynamic transformation, ending in the slumped position against the wall, looking like Lee Marvin's horse in *Cat Ballou*.

Another common courtship indicator is self-touching or preening. Much like a bird smoothing its feathers, we unconsciously arrange ourselves when we are expressing interest. As the young man above slowly stood up, he unthinkingly straightened his tie and hitched at his pants. The woman was in better control. She only smoothed her skirt three times.

In addition to preening, men will hold their head high in a proud and confident position, highlighting the neck and chin lines. Women will give the corner-of-the-eye look made famous by those TV commercial lovelies who slither around in the front seat of a sports car. For men or women, the chest will be out and the stomach will be tensed or pulled in.

When sitting, women may cross their legs, or tuck one leg under. A women might stand with her feet in the model's T position, creating a curve to a narrow base.

In cases of extreme interest, there will be what's called a "pelvic tilt." This rocks the hips forward at the pelvic bone, causing the back to arch slightly and accentuate the stomach and the derriere. Think of the classic John Travolta pose in the *Saturday Night Fever* movie poster, or the glamor pose of a starlet on the red carpet.

As another sign, researchers have found that people's eyes will dilate when viewing something interesting. In fact, that's why tournament poker players and professional negotiators always wear dark glasses, so their eyes won't give away important information as the result of an autonomic response.

Women may indicate their interest by showing their palms in feminine gestures—from holding a person's forearm as they converse to coughing coquettishly with the back of the hand to the mouth.

Male courtship behavior is characterized by overlong gazes (immoral looking time), droopy eyelids, and a slight smile. Think of Snoopy the dog from *Peanuts,* in his "Joe Cool" persona, learning up against the wall. The chest is out, the stomach in, the chin tucked back, and the head tilted in a relaxed "agree" position. The hands are often held in a dominant and aggressive hip position or a modification with thumbs hooked in the belt or hands in pockets.

At a distance, interest is revealed by smiling, preening, and immoral looking time.

Close up, you can begin to spot NVC signs that often indicate more than just interest. A lover's look, sometimes called a "knowing glance," can pass between two people who are sharing intimacies. They may also have "lover's hands," which break the touching barriers normally present in social situations. Their touch may last a fraction of a second too long, or they may touch normally forbidden areas such as shoulders in too familiar a manner.

What's the point in all this? This is supposed to be about business, not meeting people in a bar. The issue is, problems occur when an employee is sending the wrong signals to another employee, or when an employee misreads another employee's actions. One employee thinks he or she is simply being personable and attentive. The other employee thinks that there is dating interest present. That is how harassment situations begin and escalate.

So as a supervisor, it is important to recognize such potentially unprofessional and confusing behavior when you see it. And personally, as an employee, it is important to make sure that your actions cannot be misinterpreted.

Begin to notice the courtship behavior interactions in your working environment (and socially, too). NVC can be a good cross-check against the grapevine, and it is often more reliable. At work, you are not in the "pick-up" business. But you can pick up on when there is more electricity in the air than in the walls.

Travel NVC

Traveling is one uncomfortable NVC situation after another. Even when I know what to expect, I find travel to be at least a bother, and is often downright unpleasant. The negative effects of travel are caused by the inability to adjust to a rapidly changing physical environment inhabited by strangers. The participants all become non-people because of the tremendous volume flowing through the system. As hard as the airlines try to personalize their service with nametags for their attendants, brightly designed terminal gates, and giveaway magazines, the impersonal nature of the effort remains.

You can make your travel more pleasant by analyzing what has been happening to you from an NVC standpoint. Once you understand that the sanctity of your territorial space will be violated for the duration of the trip, you will be much happier. Once you steel yourself to doing business with an array of nondescript strangers (who regard you as a stranger, too), you will be much friendlier. Once you start recognizing the NVC information that others are transmitting, you will be much more knowledgeable.

Be more observant in the terminal. When you pass a bank of seats, look at the various people sitting or standing there and see if you can tell who they are talking to, the way you did with the executive in Chapter 1.

If there are benches lining the walls or out in the open, notice how people sit at them. As with all seating arrangements, there are dominant and submissive positions. The person sitting submissively on one end of a bench is saying, "See, you can have the other end of the bench and we won't invade each other's space."

The person sitting challengingly in the middle is saying, "I dare you to sit on either side of me where there's not enough space for us to be apart."

On the airplane, watch how the attendants behave. Because attendants have to reach so much, their center is rarely opened to the passengers. They are always facing down the aisle. In addition, the seated passenger is in the awkward position of having to look up and over to the attendant with the protruding headrest bulge at his or her neck. Consequently, eye contact is brief at best. When dealing with attendants, call them by name (last name) and maintain strong eye contact. It will do wonders for your service.

Be aware of the person sitting next to you. He or she is probably just as unenthusiastic as you are about the trip. Hopefully, you don't have to play the armrest game, or deal with a knee-bumper.

If the non-people next to you show potential, try to involve them in conversation. If they don't want to talk, you will soon find out. I find that most travelers welcome conversation. I've passed some of my most interesting hours seated next to strangers on an airplane. The chances are that the people next to you will welcome a respite from the impersonality of the trip and continual assaults on their sense of space.

Watching NVC can make your trip more interesting. Using NVC principles to change what happens on the trip can make it more pleasurable. The choice is yours.

Restaurant NVC

Another common locale for business dealings is the restaurant. I always prefer to entertain out rather than at home. It never fails that when I have an important client relaxed in the living room, the toilet backs up all over the bathroom floor or the dog goes into labor. One time my automatic garage door opener broke with a guest's car inside the garage. It took me nearly 45 minutes to dismantle the attachment from the door to the track.

Another nice feature about entertaining out is that you can create the impression of high living at very little cost. You can live in a one-room apartment and drive a rust box, but if you own one good outfit you can entertain in style and never lose any social status. The only real negative is that you are no longer able to eat in privacy.

Whenever people eat in public, they pretend they have suddenly gone deaf in order to create the illusion of privacy. Even though a conversation easily carries to the next table, no one shows the slightest reaction to what is being said next door. If a group is particularly loud and boisterous, the other diners will begin glaring their disapproval at the disruption of their illusion.

If you are the one making loud conversation, be careful of loose talk. I was eating lunch once with a group of people from my office when the topic turned to one of our clients. As the client's name was mentioned in a derogatory fashion, my friend Sam nudged me and nodded toward a man at another table who suddenly looked as if he had grown rabbit ears. He could have been an extra in the classic old commercial ("When E.F. Hutton talks, people listen").

There was no way to warn the other salesperson without alerting the now-interested listener, so we quickly shifted the conversation to another subject. On the way out we told the others what had happened, and discussed the dangers of loose talk in public. It turned out that we had indeed been overheard by this customer's immediate superior, who relayed the comment directly back to the customer. It ended up creating serious tension with the account.

People often have a hard time pretending not to be listening. I once ate lunch in a customer's cafeteria and couldn't help but hear the conversation next to me. A group of executives were reminiscing about a friend who had been transferred. The one story I had the worst trouble "ignoring" concerned an unusual experience this friend had at a downtown motel in a large city. In the middle of the night, wanting to go to the bathroom, he went out the wrong door and found himself standing in the hallway in his underwear, locked out.

At that point, most of us would have curled up into a fetal ball and started crying. This executive was famous for his iron will and control of every situation. Searching the deserted hall, he found an old newspaper and wrapped it around himself, and walked the hall until finding a house phone near the elevator. The phone was answered by a laughing operator who listened to the story patiently, then commented, "I know. We've been watching you on the security cameras. A bellhop is already on the way."

The table next to me was in an uproar as the executives retold their favorite story. I was sitting next to them, twitching in my chair, choking on my food, and trying to remain stoically deaf. What made it worse was that they saw I was laughing and began to watch me pretend I wasn't listening.

The point is, the next time you are in a restaurant, observe the other diners as they silently "interact" with their neighbors. People never really eat alone. They merely don't have anyone at their table to talk to.

Restaurant owners understand this privacy problem and arrange their facilities to minimize it. The first thing they do is darken the room. Just as a theater goes dark to allow you to lose track of the people sitting next to you, so the restaurant lowers its lights to enhance the illusion of privacy. It can be overdone, though. Some places are lit so dimly that you feel as if you are eating in a submarine con at night. You stumble through your food in relative secrecy and walk out into the bright daylight snow blind for five minutes. The best level of lighting is one that is as low as possible without making customers say, "Boy, it's sure dark in here!"

Some restaurant owners try to minimize rear fear in their layouts. My local neighborhood diner recently added about two partitions to its dining room. Even though the dividers eliminated most of the eye contact between tables, they did little to create a feeling of privacy. The tables had been jammed up next to the partitions to preserve the restaurant's seating capacity. Without the partitions, the tables had at least been several feet apart. Now parties were so close that even a whisper carried past the chest-high divider. Partitions can't maintain sound privacy. They can only create physical separation.

The most common approach to sound privacy is to mask the restaurant sounds with music. Since restaurant owners do not want to waste expensive space on making people comfortable, they substitute an aural potpourri that acts like an acne cover up. It doesn't make the blemish go away. It just makes it less noticeable. After several minutes, our marvelous brain adjusts itself to tune out all the nonessential sounds and begins to think there really is "quiet"—that is, except for the kitchen.

Wherever I go I seem to end up next to the kitchen. In the event that area is mysteriously full, I am put next to the serving area, replete with spare supplies and dirty dishes. It amazes me that the same restaurant displaying Louis XV antiques will have wide swinging doors that show brief glimpses of sweating cooks retrieving half-done meat from the floor, throwing globs of salad into a bowl, and chewing on their nails. And the requisite for most kitchen help is that they be able to yell like Foghorn Leghorn, so that diners eating in elegant surroundings and atmosphere (defined as old furniture, darkness, and no Muzak franchise) hear snatches of kitchen conversation wafting past the swinging doors. Such exposure to the mechanics of feeding people can spoil even the most careful of efforts in the dining area.

Another factor that destroys privacy is people watching us eat. Many times, the worst offenders are the help. Some of the fancier restaurants will assign a busser to each table, standing there at all times. The waiter will hover nearby looking for the merest flicker of an eyebrow or a head poised to rotate in search. This type of service can be annoying at best and stifling at worst.

I may be oversensitive to it, but ever since I waited on tables in my college days, I haven't been able to view restaurant employees as non-people. I remember that my ears did not become plugged the minute my uniform went on. Much like standing in the elevator, I frequently heard interesting bits of conversation as the diners completely ignored my presence. Now I don't enjoy a meal when I know each comment is being monitored by several sets of ears.

Some restaurants compound the problem by locating the waiting area next to the dining room. This way, the clatter of hungry patrons looking at you like children peering through a pet store window becomes part of your "dining experience." I wonder if owners do this on purpose to speed the turnover, or if they are just careless. On a crowded weekend, you can feel like a depositor withdrawing savings during a bank run under the panicky eyes of those hoping to find money left when they get to the window. I would rather eat in the kitchen than near the reservations desk, hearing the poor host squeeze through the crowd and periodically shout, "Johnson party of two? Johnson party of two?"

If feeling like stuffed customer under glass isn't enough to make you speed through your meal, sitting on restaurant furniture probably will. A New York City diner called in a management consultant to help speed its turnover of lunchtime patrons, who tended to linger over their meals. The consultant suggested calling in an orthopedist to solve the problem. The owner took the advice, hired the doctor, followed the doctor's recommendations, and immediately nearly tripled the lunchtime business. What the doctor did was to redesign the seats so that they were comfortable for only about 20 minutes, the average eating time. Early arrivals cleared out before the noon rush and the noon arrivals were finished in time for a new group at 12:30 p.m.

In the typical restaurants, comfortable sitting time might range from 60 to 90 minutes. After that, the bottom begins telling the stomach that no matter how good the food and drinks are, it is time leave.

Another factor can be table design. Most restaurants prefer tables that are supported in the middle by a single pillar with a wide base. These greatly restrict the legroom underneath the table, so that it is impossible for taller diners to stretch out their legs. An hour sitting upright or with legs bent back under a chair is about all most people can endure before having to stand up. A trip to the bathroom is normally the only respite—unless you are leaving. The normal four-legged table support provides much more leg space, although it does reduce the seating options. (It also stops all those "excuse me's" generated when you step on the base thinking it is someone's foot.)

If you hope to transact some business during a meal, you should follow several rules. Unless you plan to linger at your table, you had better complete most of your conversation before the food arrives. Once everyone starts eating, the conversation will come to a standstill. Another good reason to get down to business early is that before-dinner drinks dull things a bit. If you need the relaxation, fine. If you don't, you're going to get it anyway. After dinner, the body begins to slow down in accordance with nature's plan. The stomach steals blood from the brain for the digestive process. The combination of booze dumped into an empty stomach and digesting food definitely makes Jack a pretty dull boy. Hit your topics while everyone is still mentally present.

Choose a restaurant for business meetings with care by asking yourself the following questions:

1. Does it have adequate lighting for eating?
2. Does it have sight privacy from neighbors? Help? Bar patrons? People waiting?
3. Is there acceptable sound privacy for the subject matter to be discussed?
4. Can you be assured of a table away from a noisy kitchen, serving area, busboy station, or reservations desk?
5. Is the help competent but not over-zealous or intrusive?
6. Is the furniture comfortable for the length of time you plan to spend there?

Remember that people's impression of a restaurant is more often a result of the time they had there than of how good the food was. So only when all the above questions are answered satisfactorily should you worry about the food. Quality will often vary from dish to dish, night to night, and opinion to opinion.

As the above questions suggest, you should never plan an important meeting around a restaurant you have never been in. From an NVC standpoint, good restaurants are hard to find, so begin to analyze your favorites and any new places you encounter. It's time you got more out of a meal than a full belly.

Shopping NVC

I am always put off by a store employee who says, "May I help you?" and then stands there while you look at the goods. I feel like Linus being stared at by Snoopy when he is playing vulture up in the tree by his dog house. Salespeople don't really want to stand and watch customers either, or else they wouldn't ask a question that invites a "No" response. They are like children doing school fund-raising who come to your door saying, "You don't really want any seeds today, do you?" When you agree, you can see the relief on the kids' faces as they muster their courage to go to the next house.

The problem, once again, is our difficulty in dealing with strangers. The rules of "moral looking time" tell us that we shouldn't be watched. Yet the clerk wants to be of help (or stay close enough to make certain we don't cart anything off.) We are non-people to each other, immediately placed under the headings of clerk and customer. Most of the conversation is very plastic, from the "May I help you?" to "No, thank you, I'm just looking" to "Thank you and come again" at the end of the sale.

One retail store manager told me that the best way to break this pattern is to greet the customers as they come into the store. Instead of walking up to them after they have entered the store and asking the "Help you?" question, his clerks meet each customer at the door with a "Good morning" or "Isn't it a nice day?" They then leave customers alone as they shop, returning only when it is apparent the customer is looking for a specific item or needs some help. At this point, the clerks comment about the item or ask if they can be of assistance.

The manager also mentioned that the most important employee in the store is the cashier. Many stores make the mistake of placing an inexperienced clerk at the register and handling this step as a mass-production line. Instead, this position should be reserved for the brightest and most cheerful personality on the staff. Here is the logic. The last person the customer deals with is the cashier. As the old saying goes, "You can have a bad meal, but make sure the coffee's good so people can at least leave with a pleasant taste in their mouth." The cashier can ensure that any complaints are brought to the surface and that the customer leaves with a positive feeling.

The best stores have employees who know how to be personal with customers. I once went with my wife to buy a dressy winter coat. We ended up in a small specialty shop that, in addition to women's fashions, sold the various antiques that made up the decor. The saleswoman, a native of Israel who was living in the United States, showed us how effective the personal approach could be. She introduced herself and within the first few minutes of conversation gently probed for all sorts of background information. She soon knew how many children we had, where we lived, what I did for a living, and was getting a good idea of our personalities as my wife and I talked about coats. While my wife was in the back of the store looking at collars, the security guard in the front started discussing sports with me. My wife and I ended up spending nearly 90 minutes in the store, and by that time we were considering buying a hall tree, a cuckoo clock, and an English hunting horn, thanks to the skillful guidance of the saleswoman.

Managing to halt my right hand before it could get to my wallet, I began to think about what had been going on. I realized that the saleswoman and the guard had been treating us as friends, and that we felt incredibly comfortable with them. They had burst through the artificial non-person barriers people erect for strangers, and in doing so had eliminated their own. We did buy the coat, and I'm sure we will shop in the store again, because at no time did we feel like the employees were hovering over us or pushing anything on us.

A local jewelry firm uses a somewhat different approach to break down normal sales barriers. All its stores are designed with the display cases about desk high. The stores are adequately staffed and equipped with small padded stools. When you stop at a counter to examine a piece, the clerk invites you to sit down and then unlocks the display case.

This is an excellent selling approach, because it forces the customer to relax and gives the clerk more time to sell. Once customers are off their feet, they tend to stay a while. The clerks can service more than one customer at a time as long as they leave no more than one piece out at a time. Seated customers don't seem to mind being left alone as much as standing customers do. The cleverest part of the approach, though, is the use of stools rather than chairs. The stools are designed so that customers can take their weight off their feet, but they are not really comfortable. Like the seats in the New York diner, the stools ensure that turnover doesn't suffer by letting customers get too relaxed.

Getting customers *out* of a store isn't a major concern these days. Every retail store would love to have that problem. The real challenge is to get them *into* the store. This is often done nonverbally with displays that customers see when walking by. The display must some- how say, "Buy me!" It must immediately catch the eye. And if the store is in a shopping center, it must be distinctive from other windows.

Most display windows are elevated so that the merchandise is closer to eye level. Within the store, goods placed on the upper shelves will sell better than those on the lower shelves. Just as we will write a phone number on the telephone booth wall at eye level, so we notice more when we don't have to look up or down. An old merchandising maxim states that "85 percent of the buy is in the eye." If a display can't catch the eye, it won't catch the sale.

We are also attracted by color. Displays using banners are consistently effective. Christmas windows are easy to do because the colors are bright and garish. Green mice in red stocking caps are perfectly acceptable at this time of year. Good displays involve the observer, encouraging shoppers to mentally put themselves into the scene. In fabrics, for example, where the goods anticipate the seasons by three to four months, a winter window will show a colorful spring scene, or a sunny day at the beach.

Once customers have been lured into the store by the display, advertising, or previous experience, the goal is to make them walk through the entire store. The layout can be cleverly designed to increase store touring. For example, the most expensive goods are usually placed in the front of the store. Most people will not want to spend that much money, but they will be impressed with the quality of the store and its merchandise. They will begin to work their way backward in search of more reasonably priced articles. The rear of the store is the best location for items in greatest demand. Display goods are placed here, because they will sell better than items not on display.

Specialty items should also be in the rear. For example, a fabric store that stocks hard-to-find drapery material keeps these goods in the floor area farthest from the door. The manager explains, "We're noted for our fine selection of drapery goods, so there's no reason to try to draw people in with a display or to place the goods up front where they are more likely to be seen. My customers will go wherever the goods are located. If I had a basement in the store, I'd put the drapery goods there."

Sale goods require a different approach. Sale items are sometimes placed in the rear of the store, but more often they are spread out over the sales floor. Large discount stores and department stores often send out weekend flyers showing a wide range of goods. If you bought every item in the flyer, you would have to make a complete circuit of the store.

These stores also move customers around with nightly specials announced on the PA system. Typically, the store first announces a temporary special in the rear of the store, then announces further short-term sale items located in the opposite corners. The announcement might blare out, "Shoppers, there's a puce-light special over in the Sweat Socks Department. You can get pink argyle ankle wraps for $2.95 for the next ten minutes only." The announcer then cleverly never tells you exactly where the Sweat Socks Department is so that you have to wander around the store a bit. Store directory signs are usually somewhat vague for the same reason.

Another technique to make customers tour the store is to separate the entrance and exit areas. The entrance has a one-way gate so that customers cannot leave the way they came in. The only path out of the store is through the exit lanes, which are in a different area from the entrance.

Stores are also designed to make movement from floor to floor difficult. The elevators are buried in the back of some little-traveled department such as Scouting Clothes and labeled so that you can't see them from more than a 20 feet away looking straight ahead. (This is frequently true of bathrooms, too.)

Escalators are often arranged so that you have to walk around to the other side to continue your way up or down. You are never allowed to walk adjacent to the elevator bank. Your path is usually cut off by some goods, so that you have to walk through them. Indirect pathways guide you past a number of the most interesting departments, such as women's sportswear and shoes. The specialty departments, where most purchases are planned, not impulse, are almost always located near the outside walls away from the escalators.

Departments are also arranged to fit customers' shopping patterns. Men's and women's departments are placed next to each other, so that if husbands become bored shopping with their wives (or vice versa), they can be drawn over to something that attracts their interest.

For example, a local chain store places hardware next to housewares, and calculators and sporting goods next to cosmetics. All impulse items are placed near the checkout counters or the exit walkway (with a security guard stationed there to reduce shoplifting). All these techniques are designed to get you into other parts of the store.

Within the departments, there are many nonverbal tricks to help you make the decision to buy. One of them—called "pyramiding" in the liquor industry or "stack and sell" in the appliance industry—involves displaying an enormous number of items in a "sculptured" pile. The nonverbal message to many shoppers is that if the store had enough confidence to buy in such quantity, the items must be good.

Another approach is to lay a large number of items directly on the floor, with a sign showing only the price. The informal display and lack of promotional hoopla suggest to the customer that the store is offering the items at a good price in order to get rid of them.

The layout within a department is also carefully planned to encourage you to buy. Good display space is never wasted on staple merchandise. Standard best-sellers can be relegated to the walls or placed on lower shelves, since these items do not have to be seen to be bought. In a grocery store, for example, people will go out of their way to find staples such as soups and canned fruits.

The ends of the aisles in any store are prime promotional spaces, because they are high-traffic areas. Customers pass them going up and down the aisles and walking from department to department. The most attractive, unusual, or colorful goods are placed here to lure customers over for a closer look. If a department does not have a particularly display-worthy group of goods, or if its merchandise is fairly stable (for example, small appliances), the goods are shuffled from location to location every week so that it appears, to regular customers, that new merchandise has been brought in.

Certain methods of display attract our attention. An executive for an appliance distributor told me that TVs are often displayed incorrectly. They should all be tuned to the same channel and left running with the sound off. As customers walk by the appliance department, they see a whole wall of images in synchronized motion, like a TV screen as seen through the lens of a fly.

Motion is the ideal attention getter. Paper flutters from the vent of an air conditioner. A humidifier runs off a clear plastic tank filled with goldfish, with the blown moisture collected on a glass pane and funneled into the tank below. All the clocks in the home furnishings section are set at a different time so that something is chiming, bonging, or cuckooing every few minutes. At car shows, automobiles are displayed rotating on a turntable. The sign above the bank spins hypnotically, blinking time and temperature alternately.

Touch is another important attention getter. One of the advantages of running a TV with no sound is that a customer must touch the set to try it out. Once the customer adjusts the sound, a psychological barrier has crumbled and a strange sense of ownership begins to grow because of that touch. For example, you may pass by a car you test-drove once and still think of it as "your" car. You will search a jewelry counter for a ring you tried on several months ago before you look at the other items.

One very successful pet store owner depended heavily on touch in selling. Whenever a parent and child came in "just to look," he would leave them alone, watching the child's eyes. Only after the child had locked eyes with a pet, the owner would walk up and ask the parent if he could help.

The parent would reply with something such as, "We're not buying right now. We were just thinking about getting a dog and wanted to see what you had."

The owner would stride over to the puppy the child was watching, get the dog, and hand it to the child—*not* the parent. He told me, "Once I get that puppy in the kid's arms, I'm home free. Most puppies will lick anything that moves. So there's the kid, with a squirming and licking puppy in his or her arms, looking imploringly at the parent. It's almost impossible to resist. If the parent is still unsure, I make *him or her* wrestle the dog out of the kid's arms. I don't let them get away with, 'Now give the man the dog.' Make the parent do the dirty work. That's when I step in and say something like, 'Wow, that puppy really has taken to you two.' If I can't close the sale 90 percent of the time at this point, then I'm in the wrong business."

Summary

A wealth of nonverbal information is being transmitted, received, and acted upon in almost every business-related social situation. Observe and enjoy watching men and women play the "oldest game in the world." Be aware of the nonverbal environment when you travel and dine out. The next time you go shopping, notice which techniques the store is using to motivate you to make the buying decision. There is an enormous amount of body business in social business.

CHAPTER 8

Developing an Effective Voice

AS YOU SAW IN CHAPTER 1, words—the actual content of our messages—contribute only 10 percent in the communication of attitudes. In Chapters 2 through 7 you saw how body movements and positions comprise 60 percent of attitude communication. It is now time to examine the remaining 30 percent—voice.

Voice is more important than many of us realize. President Nixon found out that there was an immense difference between reading a transcript of a conversation and hearing a tape recording of the voices. We aren't aware of listening to a good voice because it gets the job done without calling attention to itself. Only when a voice is ineffective do we notice it.

A good example is the "common person" or "celebrity" TV commercial. An immaculately dressed housewife "casually" being interviewed in a laundromat nervously drones, "I love new Green Sheen detergent. Since I started using it, my husband bought me a mink coat because he was so pleased with his underwear." Compared to a professional advertising voice, it sounds awkward, obviously rehearsed, and not very creditable.

Some people made a living from their voice. Mel Blanc, the actor who played Jack Benny's violin teacher and the Mexican visitor Sy ("Sy? Si, Sy!"), was the voice behind the Warner Brothers cartoon characters. (In the movie *Bugs Sunny Superstar*, he talked about some of the voices he was asked to do. The most difficult was having to portray an English horse neighing.)

Through the years, some actors have very effective voices for commercials. Paul Burke, William Conrad, James Garner, and David Janssen appeared both on and off camera in many TV commercials. The reason they were so much in demand is that they could control one of the most accurate indicators of feelings—their voice.

I use an exercise in my training classes to illustrate the many different meanings we can give the same word using just our voice. I invite three students to the front of the room and give them each a card with "Quiet" written on it, along with a description of how the word is to be said:

"Quiet!" (Everybody be quiet!)

"Quiet?" (Is it finally quiet?)

"Quiet." (Sigh. At last it's quiet.)

Say these out loud to yourself. See how it works? Students never have any problems identifying the three different meanings of each version just from how it is said.

In addition to feelings, voice can indicate when we are lying. For example, inventor Allen Bell developed a device to estimate whether people are telling the truth by analyzing their voice. Unlike the polygraph, the device did not have to be attached to the person. It could analyze tapes, TV transmissions, or phone conversations. Called the psychological stress evaluator (PSE), it measured certain tremors in the voice that are undetectable to the human ear. The voice produces a tremor at the rate of 8 to 14 cycles per second. When a person tells the truth, the muscles that control the voice are relaxed and produce a certain pattern. When a person lies, the effort creates stress and the pattern can be altered. We seem to have no control over this process.

Bell first tested his PSE on the TV show *To Tell the Truth* (where three contestants claim to be the same person and the panel must determine which one is not lying). Bell claimed the PSE was correct 95 percent of the time. In another trial, three PSE operators analyzed the statements of John Dean and John Mitchell in the televised Watergate hearings. Mitchell showed stress at several points in his testimony—for example, when he said he didn't think Richard Nixon had known about the break-in or cover- up. While the PSE is not suitable for legal situations, it suggests that there is a strong link between detectable vocal traits and honesty.

Dale Carnegie, in his book *How to Develop Self-Confidence and Influence People by Public Speaking*, tells us that, "We are evaluated and classified by four things in this world: by what we do, by how we look, by what we say, and by how we say it." You can improve "how you say it" by working on your voice. The muscles of the larynx can be strengthened and toned with practice.

When I first started speaking and training, I found it difficult to conduct a full day's class without losing my voice. I gradually strengthened my voice so I could do several days in a row with no problem. Getting greedy, I scheduled four days in succession one winter, two in Kansas City and two in St. Louis. Kansas City was in the throes of an ice storm, with the temperature hovering near zero. I was given a classroom next to the heating pipes, which banged with strain throughout the session. After two days of shouting over the pipes, I felt as if my throat had been dragged behind a horse, and I still had two days to go! In St. Louis, blessed with a quiet classroom, I managed to finish the two sessions without incident by using every technique I knew to project my voice with a minimum of effort. You, too, can develop control of your voice for strength, endurance, and effective public speaking.

Voice Control

We learn to control our voice at a very early age. Newborn babies are said to make thousands of separate and distinct sounds, but by the age of six months their range of sounds is usually restricted to those of their native language. English has approximately 50 sounds, each lasting approximately .15 second. These sounds are made by a combination of breathing, phonation, resonance, and articulation.

Normal *breathing* is a regular cycle of inhalation and exhalation every three to five seconds. When we intend to speak, we inhale more quickly, then exhale in a controlled manner. Anyone who has played a wind instrument knows the importance of the diaphragm in good breath control. The diaphragm is a muscle between the chest cavity and the stomach. It expands, making more room in the chest cavity for air, and contracts, forcing air outward. Trumpeter Raphael Mendez had such breath control and mastery of his instrument that he could play *Flight of the Bumblebee* through twice on a single breath!

When speaking, the air is passed into the windpipe and then the larynx for *phonation*. Housed at the point of the Adam's apple are two vocal folds that product sound. They are brought together and are set vibrating by the outgoing air. A set of incredibly complex muscles changes the length, mass, elasticity, and hardness of the folds to produce variations in pitch and loudness.

The vibrating air is next passed to the nasal passages, throat, and mouth cavities to create *resonance*. This is similar to the function of the sound box of a speaker in a stereo system. The nasal passages and mouth cavities are of different sizes and shapes and are lined with membranes of different degrees of firmness and moisture content. The size and shape of most of these passages and cavities can be adjusted to modify the voice.

The final step in the speech process is *articulation*. We articulate by positioning our tongue, teeth, and lips properly for each sound. You might say the last sentence, "We artigulade by posishning are ton, teethe, and libs proply for eedge soun." This is simply being lazy with verbal mechanics. One of the advantages of singing is that it teaches people to over-articulate sounds so that an audience will understand their lyrics. This discipline can carry over into everyday speech.

Dale Carnegie relates the story of a down-on-his-luck Englishman who was stranded in the United States with no money. He went for an interview in a worn suit and scruffy shoes, the only clothes he had. The interviewer was captivated by the man's mastery of the language. Despite his ragged appearance, his speech set him apart as someone special. Although the interviewer didn't hire the Englishman, he arranged for an interview with a business associate who did. By properly controlling your voice, you may affect people the same way.

Voice Codes

Certain sounds, like certain gestures, have universal meaning:

"Tsk! Tsk!" → Disapproval

Wolf whistle → Appreciation

"Augh!" → Frustration (Charlie Brown's cry when Lucy yanks the football away)

"Oops!" → Chagrin

Bronx cheer → Derision
"Yea!" → Cheer; approval
Boo! (whistle in Europe) → Displeasure
"Ow! Ouch!" → Pain
Snort → Scorn
Laugh → Humor

Some words function solely as sound imitators, for example: *bang, pop, pow, wham, bop, boom, crash, thud, swish, swirl.* As small children, we used to orchestrate our play with appropriate sound effects from our all-purpose vocal noisemaker. Somehow as adults, we lose this versatility and uninhibited use of our voice. We become expressive only when we are emotional, and may seldom rise to the occasion on purpose.

The more thought we give to our speech, the less expressive we become. With nervousness and anxiety, we increase our reliance on non-speech sounds, called *nonfluencies.* The most common of these is the *er-ah-um-uh* family of sounds. When we are making a difficult speech, we unconsciously increase these sounds to give ourselves more thinking time. "Well, ah, there are several different approaches to busing in the large cities which rather, er, affect student performance."

Nonfluencies are often used to keep control of a conversation. As long as there is sound coming out of someone's mouth, it is impossible to say something without seeming to interrupt. Frequently, people will indicate that they wish to continue speaking by making one of these sounds while giving other NVC signs of conversation: head up, eye contact broken, the posture unchanged. A new salesperson trying to make all the sales points before the customer interrupts will try this.

We sometimes let meaningless phrases intrude into our speech. "Ya know" seems to be one of the most popular, particularly among young people and recent school graduates. "Well, ya know, so it was a lot harder to get out in four years than with another major. Ya know what I mean?" The same goes for "like." These are two of the most insidious of nonfluencies.

It's similar to yawning. Once one person starts it, everyone is doing it. I once had a sales partner who was deeply into the "Ya know" habit. In a few weeks, I said it as much as he did, as did our support reps and our boss. We just unconsciously picked it up.

Some people interject strange noises into their speech. One of my instructors in school would suck on his upper bridge as he breathed in. Another instructor had a strange "dh" sound that interrupted his sentences. "The next topic we'll cover, dh, is managerial planning."

As we listen, we may also inject non-word verbal signals when we wish to speak. We clear our throat or "harrumph" when we have something to say. We also clear our throat if we are getting into a sensitive area of conversation.

"Did you have a nice time after the office party?"

"Well, ahem, I did stay late and had a few drinks."

In my classes I sometime have the students list and then read some of their long-term personal goals. They often read the more innocuous ones first, then signal the important ones coming up with an "ahem."

Other types of nonfluencies are *repetition* and *omission*. Repetition can take the form of a stutter or a repeated word. Porky Pig ends each cartoon with, "Th-th-th-that's all, folks!" Or we may repeat a word in the middle of a sentence. "I hope you can see, see what I mean." Sometimes we may even repeat part of a sentence. "It seems that—it seems that there is no alternative."

We can also omit part of a word, a full word, or an end of a sentence. Porky Pig may say, "Let's go to di-di-di-di–supper."

You may state, "It doesn't seem fair I should have to go!"

Someone may reply, "The reason…you'll just have to."

Another type of nonfluency is the *tongue slip*. I once told a class I completed a project in "one swell foop."

A student told me, "I haven't had much term this time."

If you have a large number of nonfluencies in your speech, you are definitely hurting your credibility and persuasiveness.

The problem with eliminating them is that, like most people, you are probably unaware of the habit, much as I was with the "Ya know" habit I picked up from my sales partner. What you can do is to set up your own biofeedback mechanism. The brain is a closed-loop system. It can send control signals, but depends on feedback from the controlled organs to make corrections.

The system I used to rid myself of nonfluencies revolved around my family. Every time I said "Ya know" at home, I asked my wife and kids to quietly say my name.

"Well, Sue, it seems that, ya know…"

"Ken."

"Okay, it seems that Bill is going to be a hard man to convince, ya know?"

"Ken."

Everyone is specially attuned to hearing their name being spoken. Saying my name was enough feedback to make me consciously aware of what I was doing.

At first, my family seemed to be doing nothing but saying my name every time I spoke. Even though I didn't have this "service" at work, I managed to rid myself of "Ya know" in about three weeks.

Don't be afraid to enlist coworkers or customers in your biofeedback program. I've seen whole offices embark on a "Ya know-icide" effort. It becomes particularly effective if you have to put a dollar into the "Ya know" box every time you use the phrase. Some groups have enjoyed a heavily funded "Ya know" party from their fines.

Once you have reduced your nonfluencies, look for them to creep back as you suffer withdrawal symptoms during pauses in your speech. Much like an ex-smoker wanting that after-coffee cigarette, you will want to fill up those gaps in your conversation with a sound, any sound. Tell your biofeedback partner to keep monitoring your speech for any irregularities.

Once you have eliminated these undesirable speech patterns you can begin to develop good voice characteristics.

Qualities of Voice

The first voice quality is *pitch*. Every voice has a base pitch, usually described as high ("Hi, there, I'm Glen Campbell") to deep (William Conrad as radio's Matt Dillon). Voice pitch changes direction with different types of sentences. Statements end with a drop in pitch, and questions end with a rise in pitch.

Try this. Say, "You've been working here for 12 years" both as a statement and a question. You can hear the difference meanings, even though the words are the same. One is a simple acknowledgment of fact. The other expresses disbelief that someone has 12 years of experience

The range of voice pitch can be narrow or wide. Most Clint Eastwood characters use a monotone with little pitch variation; Classic radio's Great Gildersleeve used excessive pitch variation for a humorous effect.

Voice pitch can also be thin, tense, or throaty. A tense voice, produced by tightening the throat, is particularly difficult to listen to. I once heard a preacher who used a tense public-speaking voice in an effort to speak louder. After the first 10 minutes of his sermon, the parishioners began to feel a tickle in their throat. Coughs of discomfort echoed through the sanctuary in sympathy for the minister's throat. Toward the end of the sermon, the listeners were offering a chorus of unconscious coughs and throat clearings in empathetic pain. The preacher was trying to speak louder in the wrong way.

Volume is the second voice quality. Varying volume to emphasize certain words is extremely useful in controlling meaning. Read the sentences below, saying the bold italic words louder, and note the changes in meaning.

I should mow the front lawn. (I should do it rather than you.)

I *should* mow the front lawn. (I should mow rather than do something else.)

I should mow the *front* lawn. (I should mow the front rather than the back lawn.)

Simple differences in volume emphasis changes everything.

We can even manipulate what people think they hear by the way we say something. In my classes I use a collection of puzzles that I call a Misdirection Quiz to illustrate how the voice can control listeners. Two samples read:

1. How many animals of each species did Moses take aboard ark?

2. When in history did California begin with a "c" and end an "e?"

But when I *say* them, though, I emphasize the following words (again shown in bold italic):

1. How many animals *of each species* did Moses take aboard the *ark*?

2. When in history did California *begin* with a "c" and *end* with an "e?"

As old as the Moses riddle is, nearly two-thirds of the class will miss it. The answer is, of course, that Moses never had an ark. (The poor fellow, every time he tried to do something with water, it went bad on him or it dried up.) Noah was the ark builder. But the emphasis on "of each species" focused attention away from the Biblical name. Listeners simply put in the name they expected to hear.

The California riddle is trickier, and few people ever catch it. The answer is "always." Reread the sentence aloud, putting emphasis in this manner:

2. When in history did **California** begin with a **c** (pause) and **end** (pause) with an **e**?

The answer is: The word "California" has always begun with the letter "C," and the word "end" has always begun with the letter "e." You see, by changing the volume of your voice (and a little bit of timing), you focused attention away from the alternate meaning of the sentence.

Volume is also a good indicator of emotional intensity. Loud people are often thought to be forceful and aggressive. Have you ever tried to fight in a whisper?

Right after we were married, my wife and I lived in a typically tiny college apartment with paper-thin walls. Everyone could hear what the neighbors were doing and saying, particularly through the bathroom. We learned to argue in a whisper that more often than not resulted in our breaking up when we showed strong body language signs with whispering voices. After we moved to a duplex with greater sound privacy, we had a terrible time learning to argue in a regular voice. (When we did, though, our disagreements were much more satisfying.)

The proper way to produce volume is not to work harder, like the preacher, but to work more effectively. This comes as a result of using the diaphragm properly. You don't have to run a large amount of air past your vocal cords to be loud. This makes you sound breathy, like a bubblehead sharing personal secrets with the world. You should push the air firmly out of your lungs with your diaphragm. My trumpet teacher would suddenly poke me there while I was playing a passage. If my diaphragm was pushing properly, the sound would continue. If I was shoving air incorrectly through the horn, there would be a blurp.

You can tell if you are using proper breath control with this experiment: As you speak loudly, loosely cover your mouth with your hand. If the sound is almost entirely muffled, you are too breathy. If the sound is only partially muffled, your diaphragm is pushing properly. Another test is to speak loudly without blowing out a match held several inches from your mouth. Volume is properly made with the larynx, a muscle that you can strengthen for louder and more sustained speech.

The third voice quality is *resonance*. Without the fullness of a resonant tone, the voice takes on a nasal quality that Dr. Bill Beeners of the Princeton speech department called "the loveless twang."

Your resonant passages can be blocked by a cold or congestion. In our family, the proof of whether you had a cold was how you said "Pat Boone." If it came out "Bad Bood," then you had a cold.

You can even purposely block off your resonant passages if you wish. Scuba divers learn to do this simply for survival. Most people breathe through their mouth and nose simultaneously out of habit. Under water without a facemask, this leads to choking and eventually drowning. So a diver is able to close off the nose when necessary, and breathe only through the mouth.

As a hay fever sufferer, I often ran into the problem of having to give speeches when I was congested. I sounded blocked a good portion of the time, especially in the summer. To solve this problem, I practiced my presentation on a tape recorder, using the scuba-diving trick to teach myself to speak without nasality.

When you have a cold, or if your voice sounds as if it is coming out of your adenoids, you can try one of these techniques to improve your vocal image. First, speak more slowly and over-enunciate. When I spoke at normal speed or even faster when I was congested, I tended to mumble with lack of resonance. When I felt I was speaking ridiculously slow and enunciating as if I were a diction teacher, my voice sounded fairly normal.

Second, let the pitch of your voice play a more important role in your speech. Raise your base pitch a tone or two, and increase your pitch range. This will help restore some of the expressiveness to your voice and will draw attention away from your clogged sinuses.

The final voice quality is *tempo*. We can speak quickly or slowly, fluidly or with hesitation. At one time or another in our careers, we have all been around the machine-gun talker. One of my favorite examples is James Cagney in the 1961 movie *One, Two, Three*. In this sophisticated Billy Wilder comedy, Cagney played a soft drink executive in West Germany who continually spewed out numbered instructions to his subordinates. The pace is so fast that you have to listen carefully to catch all the one-liners.

Classic radio comedians Bob and Ray had a routine where they parodied slow speech with an interview of the head of a national slow-talking society. The "slow talker" spoke at the rate of about 20 to 30 words per minute instead of the normal 150 words per minute. As the conversation progresses, the interviewer becomes more and more impatient, finally shifting in his chair in agony as he waits for the next word to drop. You react the same way, even as you are laughing. In my classes, I have found that speaking this slowly is third only to running my fingernails across the blackboard and using squeaky felt tip markers in irritating the students.

Fluid, continuous speech is best illustrated by those TV hucksters who do a one-minute commercial without a breath. Maybe they are selling something like the Fed 'n' Shredder, which "dices, splices, slices, spices, and ices nices twices. It will size, disguise, revise, resize, liquidize, gourmandize, oxidize, standardize, vitalize, equalize, sterilize, fractionize, tenderize, and pulverize anywise. And it costs only $11.95 plus shipping and handling with your check or money order, or $512.17 COD." After the address is repeated twice in another marathon sentence, you lean back in your chair exhausted from the blitz.

You may have also heard the typical pause-filled campaign speech delivered to a highly partisan crowd. Some political analyst comments at the close of the rousing speech, "Well, Frank, the mayor sure had the council in the palm of his hand."

To which the anchorman replies, "Yes, Henry, in a 10-minute speech interrupted only 127 times by applause, Floral Oaks Mayor Harly Goodman announced his resignation."

Often, breaks in delivery can add drama to your speech or give emphasis to certain words, such as the "pause" in the California riddle. They can make you sound as if you're making a well-reasoned, heartfelt statement.

But taken to extremes, these pauses, whether for thought or for effect, can greatly detract from your delivery. In my corporate training sessions, we retype an important speech an executive is planning to give (such as an investment broker's summary or a statement to the media) and break the speech up into the most effective voice patterns.

Quality	Male	Female
PITCH		
Base		
high	nervous, artistic,	feminine, emotional
deep	immature, forceful, mature, masculine	masculine, unemotional
Direction		
all up	nervous, high-strung	flighty, high-strung
all down	cold, unemotional, untruthful	cold, unintelligent
Range		
monotone	masculine, cold	masculine, cold
wide	dynamic, feminine, excitable	dynamic, outgoing
Quality		
thin	no significant traits	immature, sensitive, sense of humor
tense	old, stubborn	young, emotional, less intelligent
throaty	old, mature	unintelligent, cold
VOLUME		
Breathy	young, artistic	sexy, attractive, superficial
Soft	powerful	naive, emotional, feminine, attractive
Loud	aggressive, insensitive, boor	forceful, argumentative, masculine
RESONANCE		
Sonorous	healthy, energetic, proud	lively, outgoing
Nasal	many negative traits	many negative traits
Blocked	unintelligent, dull	unintelligent
TEMPO		
Speed		
Slow	careful, cold	unintelligent, lazy
Fast	outgoing, nervous, impatient	outgoing, nervous
Continuity		
Continuous	earnest, confident	confident
Broken	insincere, unsure	weak, uncertain

Table 8–1. Voice qualities and personalities traits.

President Jimmy Carter frequently broke up his sentences in unusual places, a trait that was noticed by impressionists. A typical sentence might sound like this: "It is the right of the American people... to forgo certain...luxuries much... as I do. For example, ... I don't see... Billy...as often as I should."

President Carter also had an usual habit of letting his voice drop at the end of his phrases. This hurt his image of credibility and truthfulness (see Table 8–1). The regional manager I mentioned in Chapter 4 who smiled only with his mouth also had this vocal trait. His voice merely reinforced his image of toughness and insincerity.

Table 8–1 lists different voice qualities and the images they evoke for men and women. The images are based on research from the academic literature and on the results of experiments in voice technique. In my own training sessions, I have each student tell a short personal story that is tape-recorded and analyzed by the group, which often follows the typical reactions to various qualities of voice.

Some voice qualities are open to more than one interpretation. For example, a soft voice may be regarded as either weak and feminine or very powerful, depending on other factors. Marlon Brando used a quiet, hoarse voice in portraying Don Corleone in *The Godfather*. Only people who command power and respect can afford to speak softly and slowly, making others strain to hear and wait for each word.

Less authoritative people can lose their projection of presence and power by speaking with a soft voice. When a voice quality suggests two or more contradictory traits, only the most frequently cited trait (in this case, "powerful") is shown in Table 8–1.

Voice-Quality Combinations

The real benefit of studying voice qualities is that you can learn which combinations are effective in different situations.

An interesting form of research on this topic was conducted by asking actors to read the same script to an audience using different vocal traits. The listeners were then given questionnaires to evaluate the effectiveness of the message styles. The experiment was modified and repeated several times with different audiences to verify the results.

Table 8–2 shows the best combination of voice qualities for projecting credibility, persuasiveness, and other traits. Pitch direction, pitch quality, and resonance are not included in the table, since they do not change for any of the categories. Pitch direction should always be varied, rising and dropping for each type of sentence. A normal pitch quality is always desired, regardless of the situation, as is a fully resonant or sonorous voice.

I use the credibility voice for teaching and speaking. My base pitch is normally two full tones higher when I'm talking to a class than when I'm conversing during a break. I try to make my voice more expressive by using a wider pitch range. This is not only less monotonous for the students over a long period, it also makes me sound more involved. We tend to forget that what is "too much" in a normal one-on-one conversation does not seem at all outlandish when speaking in front of even a small group. A higher base volume is also an aid in maintaining the listeners' attention. And it reinforces the speaker's passion for a subject.

Increased volume also makes a speaker's soft range more effective. Evangelist Billy Graham used this contrast to perfection, following up thundering questions with a feather-soft rejoinder.

Generally, your tempo should remain varied, again for emphasis and interest.

Trait	Base Pitch	Pitch Range	Base Volume	Volume Range	Speed	Continuity
Credibility	up	varying	up	wide	varying	less than normal
Persuasiveness	normal	varying	up	normal	faster than normal	more than normal
Cheerfulness	up	varying, mostly up	up	normal	faster than normal	normal
Satisfaction	normal	upward	normal	narrow	normal	normal
Warmth and Affection	down	slightly up	down	narrow	slower than normal	normal

Table 8–2. Effective vocal traits.

The best way to transmit credibility is to control the continuity of your speech. Well-placed pauses, together with appropriate body signals of evaluation and thought, suggest that you are a thoughtful, concerned, careful, and truthful speaker.

Contrary to what most of us think, persuasiveness is different from credibility. Although base volume should be higher for persuasive speech, pitch and volume range should be the same as in normal conversation. Persuasiveness is achieved primarily through the speed and fluidity of the message.

The stereotype of the slick-tongued, fast-talking salesman is 100 percent accurate. We have all noticed TV or radio commercials that blare out after a quieter program. These loud commercials make no attempt to be credible through varied tempos and thoughtful pauses. Instead, they focus on being persuasive, bouncing the information off us faster than we can think. We see a bewildering array of characters soaking chalk in ink, ripping shirts in half, throwing their bleach away, or talking to each other through the medicine cabinet. All these unlikely events happen within 60 seconds, yet none of the characters misses a high-paced word.

Another useful vocal trait for business is cheerfulness. When I first went into the real world as a neophyte marketeer, I asked one of the experienced salespeople in our office what I needed to become a good salesman. He looked at me for a second and said, "A thick skin," then walked off.

I soon learned what he meant: everybody loves to dump on a salespeople, because they can't fight back. On some days and in some situations, I don't feel particularly cheerful or salesy. But I know that I won't have a second chance to prove to a client or class that a poor performance was just an off day. I must always be "up." One way I do it is by psyching myself, like an athlete before a sports event. Another is by showing all the NVC signs of cheerfulness.

A cheerful voice uses a higher base pitch, with variations mostly in the upper range. The base volume should be louder and the tempo faster, with normal continuity. Volume should be within normal range. Table 8–2 also shows the best combination of voice qualities for projecting satisfaction, and warmth and affection.

Building Your Voice

Once you understand how voice qualities contribute to your image and to your effectiveness, you can begin to change for the better. The first step is to record your voice. Your phone or a low-cost digital recorder can be of value here. Try to capture your voice when you are least aware of the recorder. Most of us become automatons when faced with a microphone. Leave the recorder on during a long phone conversation or during dinner when you can forget that it's running. Have a friend record you while you are making a presentation or speaking at a meeting where there is frequent interaction with the audience. The important point is to get a sample of your normal voice.

The next step is to rate your voice for the characteristics listed in Table 8–1. Also evaluate your diction. If you are working with a friend, rate each other's voice to get a better reading. We all are so self-conscious about how we sound that it is often difficult to be honest.

Listen to your voice until it no longer sounds "horrible." I have heard myself enough times on video or audio to know what to expect, so I can now watch and listen without that self-conscious pain.

For example, in a recent radio interview about one of my clients, I experimented with using a lower pitch range. I thought the adjustment gave my voice a more authoritative sound over the radio speaker. Before, I had always sounded a little high and nervous, although I wasn't *that* nervous!

The main problem for most of us is lack of expressiveness. We speak at a consistent volume, pitch, or tempo. There is a lot to be learned from the professional voices we are exposed to each day on radio and TV. Comedian George Carlin used to joke that all the announcers sound as if they went to the same school of broadcasting.

The reason they sound so much alike is that they have all mastered the techniques of effective speaking. My favorite place to work on vocal expressiveness is in the car (difficult if you are in a car pool). I have heard some commercials often enough to know them by heart, so I announce them right along with the broadcaster. I'll come home and give my children the news and weather report in *Sesame Street* style.

You should treat your voice as another body muscle. It too needs regular exercise to stay in shape. On my way to a customer seminar,

I will warm my voice up by singing along with the radio, talking to other drivers, and thinking out loud. To work the range of my voice, I sing falsetto along with my favorite records (the "high soprano" voice for women) and sing the baseline to those pounding rhythm songs. I might spend a few minutes of an auto trip yelling part of my speech. Like any exercise, this is not to be overdone at the start. It took me many months before I could do four consecutive full-day sessions without losing my voice. If you feel a strain in your voice, stop.

Summary

Your voice is one of the most valuable NVC tools you possess. Start analyzing the voices of other speakers and try to determine what makes them expressive or persuasive. Acquaint yourself with your own voice. It shouldn't be a stranger to you when you hear it. And it certainly should not make you wince. Then, much like a singer in training, extend your vocal capabilities through practice. For the first time, you will begin to manage the other 30 percent of NVC for your benefit.

CHAPTER 9

Politics and Image

MOST OF US UNDERESTIMATE the importance of a good professional image. Politicians are one of the few groups to understand and control image successfully. Rarely is appearance such an important factor as in getting someone's vote.

People can be emotional or illogical in their voting patterns, for example, with candidates at the top of the ballot having a better chance of getting elected than those at the bottom. Americans also seem to shy away from the unusual. A candidate named Grableskew Hraboff is a longshot to win the alternate dogcatcher post. Adlai, Hubert, Wendell, Alf, and Strom have little chance against the likes of Harry, Jack, Dick, and Jimmy. A candidate who looks like he lives under a bridge and eats travelers has a lower chance of getting the nomination.

The importance of appearance was reinforced for me in the 1977 mayoral election in my home town. A well-known lawyer was running for mayor on the Republican ticket in a very Democratic community. So he was a long-shot. He had received an impressive write-up in the largest local daily and was evidently well supported by his party.

When I mentioned his candidacy to one of my in-laws, she immediately asked, "Is he good-looking? I mean, what kind of image does he have?" She was not asking for her voting information. She was *assum-*

ing that he needed a good image to have a chance at being elected. A good public image is now a prerequisite for success in politics. I doubt that someone like Abraham Lincoln could make it today. Who wants a President who looks like the "before" in a Charles Atlas comic book advertisement?

Today TV plays a critical role in a presidential campaign. Imagine going into a TV debate that will influence an election in one of the most powerful nations in history. You will command a mighty army. You will serve over hundreds of millions of people. Running for the office is the result of countless lesser attainments, years of detailed planning. Few of us will ever face an event with as much personal career significance, where so much lies in the balance. The true effect of TV on a presidential election wasn't fully realized until after the ground-breaking 1960 Presidential debates.

The 1960 Kennedy-Nixon Debate

This election pitted two experienced pros in a very tight race. Kennedy was the silver-spoon candidate, born to wealth and committed to public service. Nixon was the boot- strap candidate who fought his way to national prominence. Both understood the importance of the debate and worked hard to win it. But the results of the debate were startling to the American people and devastating to Nixon.

It was all about the visuals. A survey taken after the debate showed that people who *read* the transcript or *heard* it on radio felt it was a draw, or else gave Nixon a slight edge. But those who *saw* the candidates on TV—the vast majority of voters—felt the debate was a clear win for Kennedy.

A follow-up poll the viewers, "How did the candidates live up to your expectations for the debate?"

The results showed that Kennedy and Nixon stayed even in being as concise, fair, and as articulate as expected. But Kennedy was rated as more interesting, sharp, active, strong, colorful, handsome, relaxed, calm, deep, experienced, wise, and virile than expected. Nixon appeared more boring, dull, passive, old, weak, colorless, ugly, tense, agitated, shallow, inexperienced, foolish, and sterile. Yet both men were trying to maximize the impact of their appearance!

This debate has become one of the most highly studied media events in history. Its surprising results are the result of a complex

Figure 9–1. Kennedy–Nixon debate.

(From Randall P. Harrison, Beyond Words: An Introduction to Nonverbal Communication, Englewood Cliffs, N.J.: Prentice-Hall, 1974, by permission)

series of unfortunate circumstances, accidents, and misdirected strategies for Nixon, and some careful planning by Kennedy. The lessons learned have been applied by candidates in every debate since. Here is what happened:

The campaigning right before the debate had been difficult for Nixon. Because he was behind schedule, he spent the entire day of the debate speaking in Chicago before hostile Democratic crowds. In addition to fatigue, his health had been a problem. He had recently been ill, had lost weight, and was bothered by a knee injury. Kennedy, in comparison, had just completed a California campaign swing and was fit and rested. He spent the day of the debate in a hotel suite planning strategy with his advisers.

The TV producers did their best to guarantee the candidates equal treatment. New picture tubes were placed in all the cameras for clear, sharp transmission. A solid-color backdrop was provided to make the candidates stand out on home TV screens. Small spotlights, called inky spots, were placed to shine in Nixon's eyes in order to eliminate the dark shadows caused by his heavy brows. The producers agreed not to show Nixon wiping sweat from his forehead, since that would make him appear worried or beaten. They also agreed to keep screen time as even as possible, so that neither candidate would benefit from a larger amount of exposure.

Nixon was concerned about how his beard would appear on TV screens. Nixon has light skin and a dark, heavy beard. Even though he shaved immediately before the debate, he still had a shadow. You may have heard about the "makeup" Nixon wore that night. The truth is that Nixon used aftershave powder to hide the beard shadow from the TV cameras. This also came back to hurt him.

Figure 9–1 shows the candidates as they appeared on the TV screen. I have used the appropriate NVC checklist items to highlight their appearance differences.

As you can see, Nixon's appearance suffered. Standing on one leg caused one shoulder to be lower, and his coat to wrinkle and gap in front. His weight loss made his collar gap, and his clothes did not seem to fit properly. In addition, he did not show up as well as Kennedy on the home screens because of his lighter-colored suit. This was aggravated by the backdrop, which had been drying light even after repeated coats of paint. In fact, it was still wet at airtime. As expected, Nixon sweated heavily from the heat of the lights. Unfortunately, this caused his aftershave powder to streak, giving the "smeared makeup" look that became famous and accentuating his beard further. You can see the full range of NVC differences in Table 9–1.

The media preparations, designed to be fair, only increased Nixon's problems. The backdrop was just the beginning. The new camera tubes worked against Nixon since they picked up his streaked face better and transmitted it to millions of TV viewers. The inky spots didn't do their intended job either. They had been jostled out of line by news photographers milling about the stage before the debate began. Nixon still had those deep, sinister eye shadows the political cartoonists loved. There was even one live shot of Nixon wiping his brow, although it was from a distance.

Nixon also gave the impression of being in accord with Kennedy. Many of us unconsciously nod our head as we listen, as if to say, "I hear you." On TV, reaction shots made Nixon look as if he were *agreeing*. Kennedy shook his head "No" and took notes, supposedly to be used later.

An exposure count showed that Kennedy was getting more shots and screen time than Nixon. Yet Kennedy's advisers griped about

NVC Cue	Kennedy	Nixon
HEIGHT MIGHT	JFK was taller, although this was negated by the TV coverage.	RMN was slightly shorter, but this was not noticeable and had no effect.
SIZE PRIZE	JFK had a muscular body style. He looked healthy and fit and wore a well-tailored suit.	RMN looked tired and under normal weight. His suit fit looser than normal because of his recent illness.
HEAD	JFK shook his head as he listened, as if disagreeing with RMN's comments.	RMN unconsciously nodded his head as he listened, in apparent agreement.
Forehead	JFK had a narrow forehead.	RMN had a wider forehead due to his receding hairline.
Brows	JFK had "medially downturned" brows, giving a concerned look to his face.	RMN had dark, thick brows, giving him a brooding, negative, frowning look.
Eyes	Heavy-lidded.	RMN had deep-set eyes, which caused dark shadows under his eyebrows.
Lips	JFK had a fuller, sensitive lower lip.	RMN had downturned lips, giving the impression of a frown; deep lines from nose to mouth corners accentuated his negative look.
Chin	JFK had a square, solid jaw.	RMN had a jowly chin, which was more noticeable when he spoke.
Skin	JFK was tanned from his West Coast campaign.	RMN was light-skinned; his beard showed in blotches despite the powder.
Hair	JFK had a softer, fluffy hairstyle.	RMN combed his hair straight back in a style close to the head; his hair shone.
POSTURE	JFK stood erect.	RMN leaned to one side.
HANDS	JFK used his hands when he spoke and took notes when sitting.	RMN gripped the podium tightly to help maintain balance when standing and sat holding his sore knee.
LEGS	JFK used an open stance, weight distributed evenly on both legs.	RMN stood on one leg, resting his knee, and crossed his legs when sitting.

Table 9-1. NVC Cues, Kennedy–Nixon debate.

it to the director in real time during the debate. Yes, *griped*! They complained, "Keep the camera on Nixon. Every time his face appears he loses votes." And he did lose votes. He lost enough votes to swing the election to Kennedy's favor, a result ranked as one of the major campaign blunders in campaign history.

Even though both men were trying to maximize their appearance and had enormous resources of talent and money to help them, only one was successful. In view of the NVC data being sent out by the candidates, it is little wonder that those who saw the debate felt so differently from listeners and readers. These lessons were not lost on later candidates.

The 1976 Carter-Ford Debates

The results of 1960 were on the minds of the two candidates in the 1976 election. When Jimmy Carter agreed to debate Gerald Ford, many questioned Carter's wisdom because of the tremendous lead he held in the polls. But 1976 was a curious campaign year. Neither candidate generated much enthusiasm with the voters. Both were said to lack the personal charisma of a Kennedy or the political savvy of a Johnson. The issues were fuzzy in a down economy, and neither candidate was willing to risk being the first one to offer solutions. The arguments of "Why I was a good President" versus "Why I'll be a better President" excited no one. More than any other election since 1960, image alone may have decided the winner in 1976.

At the time, I was doing presidential debate analysis on-air for the local ABC-TV affiliate's news team, so I studied the debate carefully before, during, and after.

After the debate, a Gallup poll conducted for *Newsweek* magazine asked 517 registered voters across the country who saw all or part of the second debate, and found the results in the Table 9–2.

I believe the NVC information these two candidates transmitted in the debates explains the results of the poll and, ultimately, the choice Americans made for their President.

Neither candidate made Nixon's mistake of campaigning the day of the debate. Both prepared in detail in hotel rooms beforehand, memorizing tremendous amounts of information for the debate. Indeed, one of the main reasons each debate was limited to a single topic was to give the candidates this opportunity to stockpile information. We

	Carter	Ford	Neither or Not Sure
All things considered, which man won the debate, Carter or Ford?	50%	27%	23%
Do the following statements apply more to Carter or to Ford?			
1. Seemed well prepared and well informed	42	38	20
2. Seemed nervous and unsure of himself	27	38	35
3. Would be honest and open with the public about his foreign policy	48	33	19
4. Would have good judgment in a time of international crisis	33	45	22

Table 9–2. Gallup/Newsweek poll, Carter-Ford debate.

will never know how much of what they memorized was actually used.

Coming into the debates, each candidate had a carefully established image. Ford was the tall, rugged former athlete carrying the power and prestige of the presidency on his broad shoulders. The last two Presidents had aged terribly in office. Ford was the picture of good health after his first year. He was the only one of the previous three Presidents to leave office without being physically and emotionally drained. As the picture of Carter in Chapter 4 shows, Ford may be the only one of the last *four*.

One of my favorite pictures of Ford in office is the one taken when he received his injection during the ill-fated swine flu vaccination program. The picture showed Ford, sitting with his shirt sleeve rolled-up and a needle going into his arm, smiling at the doctor. How many of us even *look* while we get a shot? How many more of us don't flinch? Although I don't know the exact circumstances, there probably were dozens of photographers standing around Ford as he received his shot, praying for the slightest show of discomfort. Then they could blast the embarrassing photo across the country. (Remember the famous Ford ski fall shown on national evening news one winter?) Surely the President of the United States could afford to have a pressure gun used for his injections. No, Ford showed he could defy fear and look a needle in the point, smiling. Whoever set up the swine flu shot knew how to make President Ford look tough.

Carter had a warmer and more sensitive image than Ford. Publicity photos showed him carrying his own clothes on trips, reading the Bible at Sunday school, lounging in blue jeans, and being interviewed in an open-collared shirt (as in the *Playboy* magazine feature.) Portraits by Avedon of both candidates when they were asked to pose standing showed Ford stiffly upright, while Carter was relaxed with one hand in his pocket.

Figure 9–2 shows four typical pictures from the second debate.

I have once again used NVC checklist items to identify the different NVC information that the candidates transmitted as shown in Table 9–3.

As the *Newsweek* poll showed, both candidates seemed equally well-informed to viewers. But Carter seemed much more confident. He also gave the impression of being more honest and open with the public about international policy, a sore point with the American people after the Nixon administration. Yet the viewers polled felt Ford would have better judgment in times of international crisis. Here was a tough man of positive action. As a sign in every football locker room says, "When the going gets tough, the tough get going."

Both men were well-dressed. Neither made Nixon's mistake of wearing a suit that didn't show up properly against the backdrop. Their clothes were well tailored and performed perfectly. That is, they gave the candidates a professional image without drawing attention to themselves.

I was teaching a public speaking course at the time of the second debate. I asked my students to watch the debate and mentioned that I would quiz them on the delivery of the two men. One of the questions I asked was "What color suit and tie was each man wearing?" Not one student could answer, which is the ideal result. Both candidates' clothing looked professional, but didn't attract attention to itself.

Both candidates were also well-prepared, almost too well-prepared. Their delivery was about as off the cuff as a computer's. Much was made in the media about the time they spent in their hotel rooms

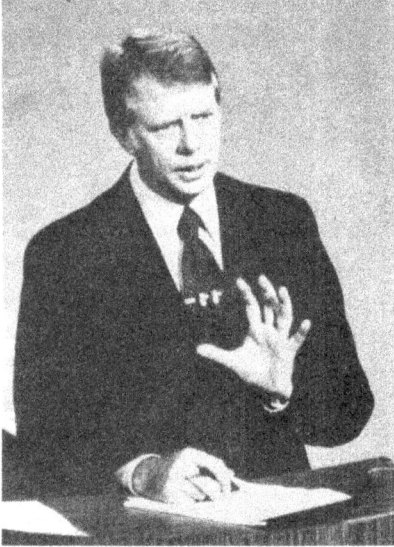

Figure 9–2. Second Carter–Ford debate.

(Courtesy Newsweek/Wally McNamee)

before each debate, and about who came and went and what they added to the discussion. This extensive preparation may have robbed each candidate of his spontaneity and image of conviction. At times the two seemed to be in a statistics duel.

In seeming more honest and open, Carter had many advantages over Ford. Carter carried himself in a much more relaxed manner. He stood comfortably, sat when listening, kept his hands resting on the lectern, and kept his center open. Carter also has a "softer" face. His fluffier hair texture and style, bushy eyebrows, open eyes, thicker lips, rounder face, and coarser- looking skin help make him look people-oriented. He is also blessed with the Kennedy-shaped eyebrows of concern. His habitual hand movement—the preacher-like palming gesture—made him appear concerned, friendly, and relaxed.

Ford was very much the opposite. He was rigid and tight in his stance, and never sat down, even during technical difficulties in the TV coverage. He made forceful edge-of-hand or pointing gestures. He closed his center off with his arms when listening, and gripped the lectern tightly when speaking. His face showed strength of purpose and resolve. His combed-back hair emphasized his forehead. He stood with square jaw, lips compressed. Here was a man of resolve and action.

Both men also seemed to learn from the mistakes Nixon made while listening to Kennedy. Ford stood with shoulders facing Carter, head cocked in an evaluative listening pose, a slight frown on his face. Carter tried a much more dangerous strategy—the slight smile.

Beforehand, political analysts had questioned Carter's wisdom in debating an incumbent, because of the limitations on criticizing a sitting president. Carter could not show a lack of respect for the office of the President of the United States, nor could he be derisive. Instead, he used an understated smile that suggested, "The current President is doing it again. Let me just have my turn and I'll show people what's wrong with that." The smile conveyed an "I've got him now" or "He's playing right into my hands" attitude.

Whereas Ford showed with his pose that he was not in agreement with Carter, Carter showed disagreement plus the hint that he had a better answer. He looked *eager* to stand up for his rebuttal. Someone should have clued Ford in on his center. If he wanted to look truly

NVC Cue	Carter	Ford
HEIGHT MIGHT	JEC is of average height.	GRF is four inches taller.
SIZE PRIZE	JEC is fit, with average build showing in a suit.	GRF, former football player, "could still hike the ball and fire off the line at Michigan."
CENTER	JEC kept his center open when talking and turned to Ford when listening.	GRF kept his center open when speaking and listened with closed center.
HEAD	JEC spoke with head tilted, "looking up" to camera; he listened with head tilted.	GRF spoke with head held straight and listened with head tilted away.
Forehead	JEC has normal-sized forehead and wears hair down over one side, a loose strand occasionally falling forward.	GRF has receding hairline, shows large forehead, and wears hair back.
Brows	JEC has bushy brows with vertical "concern wrinkles."	GRF has pale eyebrows, set close to eyes.
Eyes	JEC has wider eyes, outside corners turned down.	GRF has narrow, squinty eyes, often slitlike.
Lips	JEC has thicker lips, slightly downturned in resting position; prominent lines connect nose and mouth corners. He listened with slight smirk.	GRF has thin lips forming tight, level line in resting position; he has a toothy grin that could be interpreted as a grimace. He listened with a tight frown.
Chin	JEC has rounded, slightly jowly chin.	GRF has square jaw, that looks firmly set even at rest.
Skin	JEC's skin has a rough, almost grainy look.	GRF's skin seems smoother; fine wrinkles at jaw, around eyes, and along forehead.
Hair	JEC has coarser hair, arranged slightly over the ears; temples are silvered.	GRF wears his hair straight back in slick look; hair is off ears.
POSTURE	JEC looked more "back on his heels" than GRF. He stood upright but relaxed, and sat down when listening.	GRF looked "up on his toes." He always stood perfectly upright and squared to the podium.
HANDS	JEC held a pen in his right hand and rested it on the lectern; his left hand made palming gestures and rested on his leg when he listened.	GRF's left hand gripped the lectern tightly; his right hand made frequent gestures. He crossed his arms when listening, with hands open.

Table 9–3. NVC cues Carter-Ford debate.

negative, he shouldn't have turned toward Carter. Looking over his shoulder would have been more effective.

Both men also adopted Kennedy's strategy of taking notes during the debate. Carter took notes in a normal manner, as Figure 9–2 shows. But Ford used a curious technique. Often he didn't even look down while he wrote. Very few people can take notes without looking at the paper. In my career I have met only one person who did this regularly, a personnel manager for a large company. She wanted to maintain eye contact with the prospective employee during the interview, so she developed the habit of writing things down in very large script, using an entire page for about five lines of information. This way she could write legibly without having to look at the paper.

Ford may also have developed this skill, but it was difficult to tell from the movement of the pen whether he was actually writing or not. Also, he never once looked down at his jottings during his rebuttal of Carter's remarks. So the whole thing looked questionable, like it was a ploy. It is possible that Ford was taking notes only for show, following instructions from his advisers. "Hey, Jerry, take notes, big guy. It worked for Kennedy and it looks good."

The *Newsweek* poll made it fairly clear what the American people were looking for in their President. Carter was declared the winner by nearly a two-to-one margin.

Ford might have been more successful if he had changed his style a bit to soften his image of physical strength and force. He could have softened his gestures during the debate using fewer chopping motions. And he should have released his death grip on the lectern. This is one of the first habits to break in any beginning speaker.

Carter played the smile perfectly. No one was unhappy with his treatment of the president. He could have appeared stronger, at times standing up straighter and gesturing forcefully, with more edge-of-hand and pointing movements. It is not surprising that, two years into Carter's presidency, the major criticism of his administration was the perceived lack of direct, decisive leadership.

Both men hurt their image with their delivery. They spoke in slow, exaggerated tones, as if they were in front of 2,000 people at a political rally and needed to make up for the sound lag. Speaking before a TV camera is much like conversing one-on-one with an individual. A TV speaker is really addressing people seated ten feet away in easy chairs. Ford and Carter should have backed off the public speaking techniques and spoken on a more personal level. During the vice presidential debate both Mondale and Dole used this personalized approach effectively.

You may never face a situation with as much at stake as a presidential candidate, but your image is just as important to your career. The first impression you create at a job interview is often the determining factor in an employer's hiring decision. As you progress in your organization, you have more time to establish yourself both through your accomplishments and through the image you project to others.

Building a Successful Image

An image is a difficult intangible to manage. You can't grab it, beat it, talk to it, or comfort it. You probably can't even get two people to agree on what your image or anyone else's is. So most likely you have no idea what kind of image you project, much less how to improve it. For that matter, do you even have an image? Do you have more than one image? Are they similar or do they conflict?

The first rule in successful image building is to be *consistent*. Nobody really likes the unexpected. What does your heart do when you are surprised? It gets mad! It beats in a sprint, pumping blood quickly through your body in case you have to take action. Let someone sneak up on you and startle you, and your muscles will briefly go into seizure, followed by your heart blowing its top. Even when the surprise is pleasant, your body goes through this process.

Management is a lot like your heart. It absolutely hates surprises. A manager once told me that he didn't care what kind of difficulties his people got into as long as he knew what was going to happen. What is known, even if unpleasant, can be managed. What is unknown can be grounds for dismissal.

For managers, the worst kind of subordinate is an inconsistent one. A good performer is rarely monitored. A poor performer is constantly monitored, and needs to be. In either case, management at least knows where it stands. But nothing is more annoying to a manager than having to check up on someone who might foul up, and then discovering that the checking was needless. It's equally upsetting to have to deal with the inconsistent subordinate's personality. Is the subordinate going to be in a good mood today? Or is there going to be anger or tears?

The same is true of images. Most managers prefer employees whose personality traits can be easily identified. If a subordinate is very inconsistent, the manager becomes wary and guarded, fearful of a potential surprise. You have probably heard someone say of an associate, "He's a strange one. I just can't get a handle on him." This is worse than having negative personality traits. No one personality characteristic is inherently good or bad. Its desirability depends on the job. What may be poor in a salesman may be of value in an office manager. If you have *no* obvious characteristics, management has no basis on which to judge you for any job.

So avoid surprises in building your image. Your image should be obvious as well as consistent. This way, the people who make the decisions that affect your career will have something to count on, something predictable. They can then pick and choose among the jobs that are best suited to your traits and that offer you and the company the best chance for success.

The next rule in image building is to make your traits *harmonious*. A sales rep I know has a card that lists him as an office products salesman and a marriage counselor. Whaaat? (I've always wanted to have a card that read, "Dr. Ken Cooper, Neurosurgery and Janitorial Supplies"). It is very difficult to carry off a two-sided image—such as being hard-nosed with money but free-wheeling with ideas, or being a smooth talker but shy. The traits you choose to emphasize should agree with each other and fit together in a logical pattern.

People tend to think and talk in clichés, so the closer your image is to a stereotype, the easier it will be to establish that image. A personnel manager for a large chemical company claims she can always recognize one type of person by sight: the slick, personable, attractive office products salesperson. She feels they all look the same, talk the same, and act the same. It is unlikely that vendors are *that* good in selecting a certain type of person for its salesforce. Still, the candidates selected quickly fit into a stereotyped pattern of what an office products salesperson "should be."

If you want a nonstandard image, be careful to make your traits fit logically. In this case though, make certain that you don't come too close to a clichéd image, because that will undo all your efforts to be different. Many an office oddball has found that they are "just like so-and-so," even though the similarities are superficial. Make certain the cliché isn't still there working with you.

The most important rule in image-building is to *be yourself.*

As you grew up, you undoubtedly met people you admired and respected. You spent much of your time pretending to be these people and acting out their lives. As an adult, you must take your own talents and traits and maximize them, not try to acquire the traits you see in others. How many people do you know who are "wasted" in their current jobs or are trying to be someone they are not?

Phonies are easy to spot. Today's young people are particularly adept at sizing up others. If we try to be something we are not, it will be incredibly obvious. If we really had enough talent to keep a fake image alive, we would be actors and actresses instead of business-people. Since we aren't entertainers, we had better stick to being ourselves.

That still gives us a lot of latitude. Everyone has many different personalities, with many different traits. Dr. John G. Geier, a consulting industrial psychologist, believes that managers have three separate personalities, defined by how they view themselves, how they feel others view them, and how they act under pressure. Each of these personalities has four major dimensions: dominance, influence, steadiness, and compliance. Geier developed a test to measure these traits in assessing a manager's style and effectiveness. His analysis may be overly restrictive in the personality traits considered, but it does illustrate our varied selves.

We may also have work, spouse, and parent personalities. In fact, we may have a separate personality for every role we play. One of my customers was a particularly hard man to deal with. He was secretive and continually kept me in the dark about what was happening in the account. Consequently, I was regularly surprising my boss with unsuspected problems.

As I built up a picture of this customer as a paranoid, power-hungry sneak, I also began to learn about him outside of work. He was a warm, loving father and husband. He had many creative hobbies and was quite friendly and pleasant when he left work. He would have been a much better manager if he had let some of these traits carry over into his workday.

You are most likely the same way. You have many different person-alities, depending on the environment and whom you are with. Some-times your personality is mood-dependent: there is a "happy you" and a "down you." Out of these different selves is the making of a success-ful "you" that can be projected as your business image.

Define Your Image

The first step in building a successful image is to determine what your current image is. You may not be aware of your image, or you may think others don't have an image of you. You are wrong! Picture your friends and associates. As you think of a name, you suddenly get an image of that person. You could give a short summary of his or her personality traits. You may guess fairly accurately at how your friend would react to a certain situation or reply to a particular question. If you can do this with others, they certainly can do it with you. The challenge is to develop an accurate picture of yourself as others perceive you.

Many organizations use employee 360-degree surveys to help managers get a handle on their image. One large corporation conducts training classes after managers have been on the job three months, and then again after 18 months. A detailed (and confiden-tial) employee survey is used as a training and evaluation tool in both sessions with comparisons made between the survey results. This provides valuable feedback to the new managers.

The manager who is not offered such a program must do a little more detective work. You should start by finding out what traits you transmit to others and why you project these traits. You should be able to get an initial assessment from your spouse and close friends. Let them relay what people have said about you. Frequently, admin-istrative assistants are a good source of information, since they are often privy to conversations in the boss's office.

Ask your manager what he or she thinks of you and why. This is a valid question and can provide useful feedback on both your perfor-mance and your image. Be open-minded, and don't become defensive. Remember that the opinions expressed about you are *always* valid, if only because the other person feels that way.

Once you have an accurate picture of what others think of you, you can begin your self-analysis. In Chapter 3 you read about envi-ronment and physical appearance. You can now evaluate these two

NVC indicators as if you were a presidential candidate designing or improving a public image.

Stand at the doorway of your office or work area and pretend you are seeing it for the first time. Systematically study it (this may actually *be* the first time). Look at it wall by wall, not missing a single paint chip or ceiling tile. What do you have on the walls—paintings, plaques, diplomas, nothing? Look at the furniture. What does it say about you? Is the office sloppy, or orderly, empty or cluttered, large or small? Where is the furniture located? If you had to draw a character sketch of the person who worked in this area, what would you say? Look at other people's offices or work areas in your company. What do they have in common? What sets them apart? How does yours fit in? In other words, what is your personal work environment telling others?

What about your office attire? Even if you do not have the resources to modify your current wardrobe, you should at least become aware of how clothing contributes to your image. Does your clothing fit in with those around you? You don't have to become a fast-food clerk and show up every day in uniform, but you should know whether you are different or similar.

Is your wardrobe consistent? A salesman who was proud of his stylishness got caught one day with all his suits dirty or at the cleaners. So he pulled out an old one and wore it to work. That night, his wife came home and, seeing the suit in the wastebasket, asked what had happened. One of the salesman's customers had jokingly remarked, "I really like your suit. It's almost as nice as what they're wearing *this* year."

Are you guilty of having a "wedding wardrobe"—something old, something new, something borrowed, something blue? If you are, you will surely look like it. You don't have to keep up with fashion's every whim. But make sure your wardrobe says what you want it to say about you, and that the statement is not conflicting.

Now look at yourself. You know how to analyze your body type. You should also analyze your face. What is its resting position? Are you frowning, neutral, or smiling? Are some of the people you observe usually frowning slightly? Considering the amount of time your face spends in resting position, and decide what your "listening face" will be. It is no wonder that this characteristic can strongly influence your image.

Another important part of your image is your attitude. One of the most basic of human needs is the need to be recognized. This is particularly true in the business world, where our feelings of self-worth so often depend on the feedback we receive from managers and associates. In transactional analysis (TA) theory, the process of recognizing others is called *stroking*, and a unit of recognition is called a *stroke*.

There are positive strokes and negative strokes. Companies and organizations use awards to motivate their people ("M&M's" when the normal method, money, is not available). The training director of a large international organization talked about the problem of motivating leaders who held their posts for a single year. "We use an intricate series of awards," she said, "to overcome the motivational problems inherent in a short-term job. This keeps the leaders working throughout the year." These rewards are all forms of positive stroking.

On the personal level, positive strokes are like coat hangers—they tend to multiply without your noticing them. Suddenly, your whole day is full of good things to say to others and nice things being said in response. A retired executive, consulting with the Small Business Administration, was asked why so many of the companies requested him by name. "There are many secrets to success," he replied, "and I was fortunate to discover one of them early in my career. While I am no more competent than many of my associates, I always try to leave the other person glad to see me again, whether it's on the street or in the office."

The secretary in a college extension office was the opposite, a constant source of negative strokes. She always complained about her boss, the professors, and the working conditions. She couldn't understand why the people around her weren't more pleasant and cooperative. The most positive comment she could make was that someone had not been mean to her.

What if you were to carry a special notepad to work today? Each sheet would be divided into two columns: "plus" and "minus." For every positive stroke you gave others, you make a mark in the plus column. For every negative stroke, you place a mark in the minus column. Would your net score be above zero? If not, don't you think this is seriously affecting your image? If your score would be high in the plus column, could it be that you are a little too nice? Keep count one day, or one week, and find out how you rate.

By now you should have a better idea of what your image is. You must build a business image that is consistent, has harmonious traits, and fits your personality. In building this image, you should leave nothing to chance. Everything should be done for a reason.

Your next task in defining an image is to decide what traits you want to project. You may feel that you don't know enough about yourself to determine these traits. One way to find out is to take a battery of personality, interest, and aptitude tests. A number of psychological testing firms and consultants offer these services, but they are usually very expensive. Since many of the tests and testing procedures are standardized, you can often get similar services either free or at a low cost through an adult education course offered by a local high school.

I went through one of these courses after I left college. The first night of the program, we were given a mental ability test and then a personality inventory survey. The second night, we took vocational interest and preference tests. The third night included discussing the test results with a counselor and selecting the aptitude tests we wanted to take to investigate our areas of interest. The fourth and fifth nights involved taking the tests and reviewing the results with the counselor.

By the end of the course, we all had a much better idea of our interests and abilities, particularly of how our abilities might stack up to others' in the business world. We also had a better idea of our personalities and of what motivated us. We were fortunate, of course, in having an experienced counselor to guide us, but the test results alone would have made the course worth the time and money. The information we gained was invaluable in helping us develop an image that fit our personalities and interests.

Rate Your Traits

Based on the data you now have about yourself, you can begin to determine traits you have that are beneficial in your current job. Table 9–4 lists 325 personality characteristics. Make several photocopies, then go through the list and circle about 50 adjectives you think accurately describe you. (There are many synonyms, so don't worry about getting every version of a specific trait. That will cause too much work later on in the process.)

Obviously, your self-analysis of personality traits will be somewhat biased. If you want to get a more accurate assessment and can remain non-defensive, have your spouse, boss, and associates rate your traits for you. Then compare the items appearing on their lists with your own. You might even take into consideration the characteristics that appeared more than once on your first-impression test (Chapter 3).

absentminded	anxious	bitter	charming	conceited
active	apathetic	blustery	cheerful	condescending
adaptable	appreciative	boastful	civilized	confident
adventurous	argumentative	bossy	clear-thinking	confused
affected	arrogant	calm	clever	conscientious
affectionate	artistic	candid	coarse	conservative
aggressive	assertive	capable	cold	considerate
alert	attractive	careless	commonplace	consistent
aloof	autocratic	cautious	complaining	contented
ambitious	awkward	changeable	complicated	conventional
cool	defensive	dissatisfied	efficient	excitable
cooperative	deliberate	distant	egotistical	fair-minded
courageous	demanding	distractible	emotional	fastidious
cowardly	dependable	distrustful	energetic	fault-finding
critical	dependent	dominant	enterprising	fearful
cruel	despondent	dramatic	enthusiastic	feminine
curious	determined	dreamy	esthetic	fickle
cynical	dignified	dull	ethical	flirtatious
daring	discreet	easygoing	expressive	fluent
deceitful	disorderly	effeminate	evasive	foolish
forceful	gentle	headstrong	immature	inhibited
foresighted	gloomy	healthy	impatient	initiative
forgetful	good-looking	helpful	impulsive	insightful
forgiving	good-natured	high-strung	independent	intelligent
formal	greedy	honest	indifferent	interesting
frank	guilty	hostile	individualistic	interests narrow
friendly	handsome	humorous	industrious	interests wide
frivolous	hard-headed	hurried	infantile	intolerant
fussy	hard-hearted	idealistic	informal	introspective
generous	hasty	imaginative	ingenious	inventive
irresponsible	masculine	nagging	original	pessimistic
irritable	mature	natural	outgoing	philosophical
jolly	meek	negative	outspoken	planful
kind	methodical	nervous	painstaking	pleasant
lazy	mild	noisy	patient	pleasure-seeking
leisurely	mischievous	obliging	peaceable	poised
logical	moderate	obnoxious	peculiar	polished
loud	modest	opinionated	perceptive	powerful
loyal	moody	opportunistic	persevering	practical
mannerly	moralistic	optimistic	persistent	praising

Table 9–4. Image traits.

Now divide a sheet of paper into three columns labeled "helpful" (+), "nonessential" (0), "harmful" (-), as shown in Table 9–5. Go down your circled list of adjectives and place them in the proper column, according to how they affect your image and job success. When in doubt, place an item in either the helpful or harmful category rather than in the nonessential column.

If you end up with all your traits in the helpful column, you aren't being truthful with yourself. Your plus-to-minus ratio can be as high as two to one, with the nonessential-column size varying depending on the person and the job.

With this completed, you now have one of the most useful tools for career success to come along since having a father who is company president. The three lists should show you what to emphasize in your personality, and what to play down.

precise	quick	relaxed	rude	sensitive
prejudiced	quiet	reliable	sarcastic	sensuous
preoccupied	quitting	resentful	self-centered	sentimental
productive	rational	reserved	self-confident	serious
progressive	rattlebrained	resourceful	self-controlled	severe
protective	realistic	responsible	self-denying	sexy
prudish	reasonable	restless	self-pitying	shallow
pushy	rebellious	retiring	self-punishing	sharp-witted
quarrelsome	reckless	rigid	self-seeking	shiftless
queer	reflective	robust	selfish	showoff
shrewd	snobbish	stern	sympathetic	timid
shy	sociable	stingy	tactful	tolerant
silent	softhearted	stolid	tactless	touchy
simple	sophisticated	strong	talkative	tough
sincere	spendthrift	stubborn	temperamental	trusting
skeptical	spineless	submissive	tense	unaffected
slipshod	spontaneous	suggestible	thankless	unambitious
slow	spunky	sulky	thorough	unassuming
sly	stable	superstitious	thoughtful	uncomfortable
smug	steady	suspicious	thrifty	unconventional
undependable	uninhibited	unselfish	warm	wise
understanding	unintelligent	unstable	wary	withdrawn
unemotional	unkind	vindictive	weak	witty
unexcitable	unrealistic	versatile	whiny	worrying
unfriendly	unscrupulous	vulnerable	wholesome	zany

Table 9–4. Image traits (cont.)

Helpful (+)	Nonessential (0)	Harmful (−)
active	affectionate	absentminded
assertive	ambitious	aggressive
confident	candid	anxious
curious	conservative	argumentative
dominant	determined	bossy
energetic	efficient	demanding
enthusiastic	high-strung	forgetful
forceful	individualistic	fussy
good-natured	logical	hard-headed
humorous	methodical	impatient
informal	natural	nervous
intelligent	persistent	opinionated
interests wide	practical	reserved
inventive	sentimental	restless
original	simple	skeptical
perceptive	stable	stubborn
polished	stingy	tense
rational		worrying
self-confident		
showoff		
sincere		
thorough		
uninhibited		

Table 9–5 Sample image traits analysis for a specific job
(corporate trainer).

Keep in mind that the value of a given trait depends on the job. If you are looking to move upward in the organization, you may want to make an additional list for any positions you aspire to, especially if it involves very different success traits from those in your current job.

One of the oddities of the workplace is that people are sometimes judged more on their capabilities than on their performance. Someone that management feels is an "up and comer" may be able to explain away poor performance as "the best in a bad situation." Selling this often depends upon how well the person's "next job" image is solidified in the eyes of management. These lists can provide you with guidelines for developing not only an image of competence in your current job, but one indicating that you can do the next job as well.

Project Your Image

Now that you have a list of your desirable and undesirable traits, you are in a position to project the proper traits. This is the final and most difficult step in building a successful business image. Unfortunately, there is no well-defined system for implementing your image. Just as no two people's lists will be the same, so no two people will use the same approach in projecting an image. You have been exposed to a large number of NVC signs and techniques, covering where you put your body and what you gather around it. You can now use this information to project your image.

Start with your work area or office. If you want to convey order and precision, have all material neatly filed and labeled. Mange your time with to-do lists. Perhaps use the spiral tablet technique for note-taking. Your desk could be neat, with the drawers carefully laid out for easy search and storage.

If you want to seem busy and productive, keep your desk covered with material, with messages piled up. Have layers of file folders scattered about. Always appear to be hustling. Walk quickly through the office even if you are going to get a candy bar. There are hundreds of possibilities, all of which are correct as they are *deliberate*, and convey some trait on your list.

Make your office work to your advantage. Arrange the furniture to best fit your space needs and to gain control over your visitors. Minimize any height disadvantage by adjusting the chairs or rearranging them. Design the layout to optimize your relative physical size. Make every decoration say something about you—your personality, your tastes, your interests, or your accomplishments.

Take stock of your appearance. Is it time to get in shape? Start exercising regularly, or take up a sport. When you get your next haircut or hairstyle, go to a good professional and describe what you are trying to accomplish with your appearance. Make every purchase of business clothing fit into your long-range plan and image. Know what you want from the start and find the right look.

I can't say enough about the value of finding experienced professionals for these personal services. Even if they cost a little more, the advice they offer about style and physical appearance will more than justify the expense. We've all seen the TV experiment where a prominent designer or stylist takes a ragged member of the studio audience and returns the next week with a totally different person. That person could be you!

In his book *Winning Through Intimidation*, Robert Ringer details his methods of success in the cutthroat, high-end income-producing real estate business. When he started out, he was like every other real estate agent, working for any commission he could get from his clients. After being shortchanged time and again, he decided to develop an image that would help him get every penny of the commission he had earned.

Ringer developed an image that was so professional, so high level, that clients never thought of skipping out on his commissions. He used an expensive book instead of a business card. He traveled with his own secretarial staff and sent his assistants by airplane to fetch any documents he needed. He even walked out on one deal involving hundreds of thousands of dollars in commissions rather than fall back on his old image and agree to less than he deserved.

I once met a man who achieved success by developing the opposite kind of image. This man is one of the finest theater organists in the nation, but he has achieved national fame as a bumbling collector of antiques. You may have seen him periodically on network talk shows, displaying his oddball collection of vacuum sweepers, washing machines, and cooking utensils. What makes his visits entertaining is that these contraptions, much to his apparent amazement and confusion, never seem to work properly. The character he presents is strictly a ruse, of course.

In an interview on a local radio call-in show he mentioned that he never played the organ during his appearances. How could a confused, bumbling collector have the talent to make such beautiful music come out of a massive pipe organ? That would totally destroy his image. So he confines his organ engagements to the city where he gained fame as a musician.

It is a constant source of amazement to me that the public can accept someone who says, "Goooollly, Sarjent! Ah jist cain't unnerstan' a thang yewr yellin' aht muhee," the old Gomer Pyle character, and then sings like the leading man in a musical, who Jim Nabors really was. Yet this is the power of an image in highly visible fields such as politics and show business.

But what about the business world? When I graduated from college, I was in a quandary about what personal business style to develop.

I had accepted an offer for a position and had about two weeks to move, buy clothes, and report. A little research and questioning of people I knew revealed that the company had a conservative dress code. So I got a haircut and purchased three suits: dark green, dark blue, and dark brown. I bought five white shirts and seven striped ties that would intermix with the suits. With this dazzling array of drabness, I reported for work.

As I began my long and complex training, I could see myself fitting right into the mold. The clothing made me almost invisible, and the jargon and speech habits of the office were becoming ingrained in my conversation. People didn't work there. They were "on board." I began to think I had signed up for the Navy! My wife remarked on the change in me, not any of it necessarily bad, but a change nonetheless.

After completing almost ten months of training, I had to decide where I wanted to work in the office. Did I want to become a member of a large, well-paid marketing team, where I would be a junior member with reduced responsibility? Or did I want to get my own sales territory and have complete control and responsibility for the results? There was another factor. Up to this point, I had been exactly like every other trainee who had come through the office. If I hoped to advance in this highly competitive company, what would I have to do to shed the invisibility I had thus far maintained?

After going through the psychological testing procedure described earlier, I felt ready to begin designing my image. No matter what else, I had to prove that I was different, and that being different made me exceptional. I turned down the lucrative marketing team offer and trained for the sales position, where I would have my own territory in several years. My hair grew back to a more comfortable length, longer than most men's in the office. In replacing my wardrobe, I tried to pick suits that were much less conservative but still businesslike. Eventually, I grew a mustache, one of the first in the office.

In a town that ardently supported the local football team, I stayed loyal to the Miami Dolphins, a team I had followed since living in Florida. My desk had Pogo and Ziggy cartoons taped to it instead of family pictures. I stayed clear of office politics and avoided after-work drinking parties. When one of my managers told me I didn't fit the mold, that I was an individualist, I knew I had succeeded.

I decided to emphasize my creativity. When my unit had to sponsor a meeting for the entire office, I stayed late one night taking pictures for a humorous opening for the meeting. I also volunteered to write promotion party and meeting skits for anyone in the office. While some of these skits took lots of additional time to create, I felt that late hours were worth the exposure.

I worked at developing a reputation as a good presenter. I spent extra time preparing and reworking my visuals and delivery. I taught evening classes at a local college in order to develop a "stage personality," and I let my manager know why I was doing it. While most salesmen dreaded being assigned any in-house presentations, I sought them out as an opportunity to shine in front of my superiors.

The results may not have been due entirely to image, but by my third year out of college I was earning my age (back before double-digit inflation, and back when that actually meant something!) and had received my first title promotion, about two to three years ahead of the norm. And I was not the only one using this approach.

John C. had worked in our office for many years, but was an enigma. He was extremely well liked and competent, yet people knew very little about him outside of business. He had no outstanding characteristics or mannerisms. He had not been involved in any unusual events. When it came time to write a promotional skit for him, we were stumped, since we had so little information to work with. He had no image. Don't let that be you.

Summary

You may not have the resources of a political candidate, but you do have the same requirements for success. Take a lesson from people who are professionals at gaining other people's confidence and commitment. Define your professional image. Identify and rate your personality traits, keeping in mind their relevance to your current job and potential future positions. Then make certain you consciously project your best traits.

You can be your own campaign manager, communications consultant, strategy expert, and planner at a mere fraction of the cost a candidate would pay for those services. After all, no one knows you better than yourself. Since you know who you are, you can now use your knowledge of NVC to let others know who you are, too.

Selected Bibliography

Allport, Gordon W. (1955). *Becoming*. New Haven: Yale University Press.

Argyle, Michael, & Dean, Janet (1965). "Eye Contact and Affiliation." 28:289-304.

Argyle, Michael (1975). *Bodily Communication*. London: Methuen.

Beeners, William J. (1976). "Total Communications." Talk given to the IBM Marketing School, Endicott, N.Y., July 20.

Benthall, Jonathan, & Polhemus, Ted, eds. (1975). *The Body as a Medium for Expression*. London: Allen Lane.

Birdwhistell, Ray L. (1952). *Introduction to Kinesics*. Louisville: University of Louisville Press.

Birdwhistell, Ray L. (1970). *Kinesics and Context*. Philadelphia: University of Pennsylvania Press.

Condon, W. S. & Ogston, W. D. (1971). "Speech and Body Motion Synchrony of Speaker and Hearer." In D. L. Horton and J. J. Jenkins eds., *Perception of Language*, pp. 224-256. Columbus: Charles Merrill.

Davis, Flora (1975). *Inside Intuition*. New York: Signet Books.

Davis, Martha (1972). *Understanding Body Movement*. New York: Arno Press.

Darwin, Charles (1965). *Expressions of the Emotions in Man and Animals*. Chicago: University of Chicago Press.

Dittmann, Allen T. (1962). "The Relationship Between Body Movements and Moods in Interviews." *Journal of Consulting Psychology*, 26: 480.

Drillis, Rudolph (1958). "Objective Recording and Biomechanics of Gait." *Annals of the New York Academy of Science*, 74 (1958): 86-109.

Duncan, Starkey, Jr. (1960). "Nonverbal Communication." *Psychological Bulletin* 72: 118-137.

Eisenberg, A. M., & Smith, R. R. (1971). *Nonverbal Communications*. New York: Bobbs-Merrill.

Ekman, Paul, & Friesen, Wallace V. (1969). "The Repertoire of Nonverbal Behavior: Categories, Origins, Usage, and Coding." *Semiotica* 1: 49-98.

Fast, Julius (1971). *Body Language*. New York: Pocket Books.

Fischer, Seymour (1968). *Body Image and Personality*. New York: Dover.

Goffman, Erving (1963). *Behavior in Public Places*. New York: Free Press, 1963.

Goffman, Erving (1959). *Presentation of Self in Everyday Life*. New York: Doubleday.

Goffman, Erving (1969). *Strategic Interaction*. Philadelphia: University of Pennsylvania Press.

Half, Robert (1976). "Shorty in the Oval Office." Interview for the Associated Press, quoted in the *St. Louis Post-Dispatch,* December 11.

Hall, E.T. (1968). "Proxemics." *Current Anthropology,* 83-108.

Hall, E.T. (1966). *The Silent Language.* New York: Premier Books.

Hare, A. Paul, & Bales, Robert F. (1963). "Seating Position and Small Group Interaction." *Sociometry* 26: 480-486.

Harrison, Randall P. (1972). Beyond Words. Englewood Cliffs, N.J.: Prentice-Hall, 1974.

Hinde, R. A. (1972). *Nonverbal Communication.* London: Cambridge University Press.

Humber, Thomas, ed., & Akeret, Robert U. (1975). *Photoanalysis.* New York: Pocket Books.

Key, Mary Ritchie (1975). *Paralanguage and Kinesics.* Metuchen, N.J.: Scarecrow Press.

Knapp, Mark L. (1972). *Nonverbal Communications.* New York: Holt, Rinehart and Winston.

Korda, Michael (1976). *Power.* New York: Ballantine Books.

Lorenz, Konrad (1966). *On Aggression.* New York: Harcourt Brace Jovanovich.

Mehrabian , Albert (1968). "Relationship of Attitude to Seated Posture, Orientation, and Distance." *Journal of Personality and Social Psychology,* 10: 26-30.

Mehrabian, Albert (1969). "Significance of Posture and Position in the Communication of Attitudes and Status Relationship." *Psychological Bulletin,* 71: 359- 372.

Molloy, John T. (1975). *Dress for Success.* New York: Warner Books.

Molloy, John T. (1977). *The Woman's Dress for Success Book.* Chicago: Follett.

Morris, A. R. (1975). *A Handbook of Nonverbal Group Exercises.* Springfield, Ill.: Thomas.

Nierenberg, Gerald I., & Calero, Henry H. (1973). *How to Read a Person Like a Book.* New York: Pocket Books.

Norum, Gary A., Russo, Nancy J., & Sommer, Robert. "Seating Patterns and Group Tasks." *Psychology in the Schools,* 4: 276-280.

Pliner, Patricia, Kranes, Lester, & Alloway, Thomas, eds. (1975). *Nonverbal Communication of Aggression.* New York: Plenum.

Scheflen A. E. (1972). *Body Language and Social Order.* Englewood Cliffs, N.J.: Prentice-Hall.

Scheflen, A. E., ed. (1973). *How Behavior Means.* New York: Gordon and Breach.

Scheflen, A. E. (1965). "Quasi-Courtship Behavior in Psychological Therapy." *Psychiatry*. 28: 245-257.

Scheflen. A. E. (1964). "The Significance of Posture in Communication Systems." *Psychiatry* 27: 316-331.

Sommer, Robert. (1969). *Personal Space*. Englewood Cliffs, N.J.: Prentice-Hall.

Spiegel, John P. (1974). *Messages of the Body*. New York: Free Press.

Stanford, Phillip (1977). "A Different Lie Detector-Your Voice Gives You Away." *Parade Magazine*, January 10.

Zunin, Leonard. (1972). *Contact: The First 4 Minutes*. Los Angeles: Nash.

Index

About the Author

KEN COOPER HAS OVER 35 years' experience as a consultant, coach, speaker, trainer, and successful startup founder. He has presented over 2,500 speeches and seminars, and has been viewed millions of times by live and online clients. Ken's work has been covered by major business periodicals, written up in book form, and popularized in hundreds of radio and TV appearances.

Ken has worked with hundreds of clients such as: Apple, Anheuser-Busch, Kerry, Monsanto, Pepsi-Cola, Peoplesoft, Syngenta, Maritz, IBM, and SHAZAM Financial Network, along with numerous small and medium-sized organizations.

Ken is a recognized expert in the areas of communication and organizational development, and has created video-based online training programs for Anheuser-Busch, BizLibrary, and ej4.com. He has spoken at major industry events, worked with national political candidates, provided TV presidential debate analysis, and has made numerous media appearances discussing his work and publications.

Ken is the author of *Stop It Now: How targets & managers can end sexual harassmen*, and he is the co-author of *Taming the Terrible Too's of Training*, in addition to other books.

Ken has also written numerous articles and white papers, and has been published in *Entrepreneur, The Corporate Board, Leadership Excellence Essentials, Chief Learning Officer, Training*, and other business publications.

Read more at: www.KenCooper.com.

Dear Reader,

THANKS SO MUCH FOR reading *Body Business*. I hope that there's now a new depth and richness to your business interactions.

It's all about continuous improvement. If you enjoyed this book, please consider posting a review online at your favorite store site. Even a few sentences are greatly appreciated.

Through the years, this has been my most popular topic. It's engaging, widely applicable, and can be tailored for a number of different purposes such as personal productivity, customer service, sales, leadership, and so on. If you're looking for a speaker or trainer, this can be a fun after-dinner speech, a keynote, or a full workshop.

I'd love to hear from you. E-mail me at **info@kencooper.com** and check out **www.kencooper.com**.

– Ken

www.ingramcontent.com/pod-product-compliance
Lightning Source LLC
Chambersburg PA
CBHW060551200326
41521CB00007B/551